J. C.
Penney

Golden Rule Boy

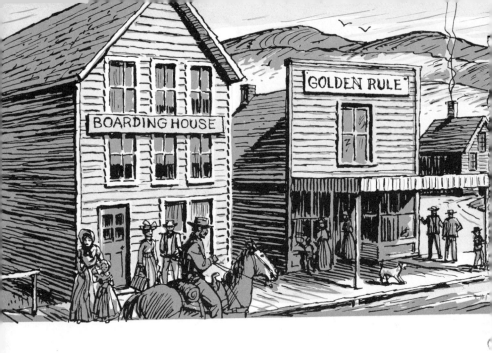

Illustrated by Robert Doremus

J. C. Penney

Golden Rule Boy

by *Wilma J. Hudson*

THE **BOBBS-MERRILL** COMPANY, INC.
A SUBSIDIARY OF HOWARD W. SAMS & CO., INC.
Publishers • INDIANAPOLIS • NEW YORK

LIBRARY OF CONGRESS CATALOG CARD NUMBER: 79-187335

PRINTED IN THE UNITED STATES OF AMERICA

*To my aunt Hattie Jones, who actively manages
Jones Brothers, the dry good store established
in 1904 by her brothers Tim and Will.*

Acknowledgments:

The author wishes to express her gratitude to Mrs. J. C. Penney and to Miss E. Virginia Mowry, Executive Secretary to the late Mr. J. C. Penney, for their gracious assistance in providing valuable material. She wishes also to thank the following for their help in research at Hamilton, Missouri: Mr. James Hill, Mr. and Mrs. George Dodge, Mr. M. O. Ridings, Editor, and the staff of the *Hamilton-Advocate Hamiltonian;* and to the following for their personal reminiscences: Mr. Paul Kennemer, Mrs. Richard L. Robinson, and Mrs. J. W. Asher. Sources of factual information included *The Dynamo* and advertising material of the J. C. Penney Company and *Fifty Years with the Golden Rule; Lines of Layman;* and *View from the Ninth Decade* written by Mr. Penney and *J. C. Penney: The Man With a Thousand Partners* and *Main Street Merchant* written partially by Mr. Penney.

Illustrations

Numerous smaller illustrations

Contents

Books by Wilma J. Hudson

DWIGHT D. EISENHOWER: YOUNG MILITARY LEADER

J. C. PENNEY: GOLDEN RULE BOY

★ # J. C.

Penney

Golden Rule Boy

Bluegrass Farm Fences

"COME, JIMMY, help me hitch old Ned to the cart," Mr. Penney called from the back yard early one morning. "It's getting late, and we have a big job ahead of us at the farm today. If you hurry, I might let you go with us."

Jimmy, almost five years old, rushed down the back porch steps. "All right, Father," he answered. "What do you want me to do?"

"Just hold up the shafts of the cart while I back old Ned into place," replied Mr. Penney. Jimmy lifted up the shafts, and Mr. Penney added, "Good, you're still only a little fellow, but you're learning to be a fine helper."

It was a hot morning in August, 1880. The Penney family lived in Hamilton, Missouri, and owned a farm, called Bluegrass Farm, about two and one-half miles away. Jimmy's father, James Cash Penney, had grown up in the country not far from Hamilton. His mother, Mary Frances Paxton Penney, had been born hundreds of miles away in Anderson County, Kentucky. Mr. Penney had first met her when she had come to visit relatives near Hamilton.

At the outbreak of the War between the States, her parents had wanted her to return to Kentucky as soon as possible. Her relatives had asked young Penney to accompany her to make sure she would make the trip safely. After he had reached Kentucky, he decided to stay there because he had fallen in love with both the bluegrass country and the beautiful young lady.

Soon he and Mary Frances had been married and had set up housekeeping in Kentucky.

12

While living in Kentucky, their two oldest children had been born, a daughter Mittie, now eighteen years old, and a son Elie, now fifteen.

After a few years, Mr. Penney had brought his family to Bluegrass Farm near Hamilton, Missouri, to live. In Missouri six more children had been born, Mollie, twelve, James Cash, almost five, Mattie, only one year and a half, and three other children who had died when they were still quite young.

The family had moved from the Bluegrass Farm to Hamilton, where the children could attend a better school. Mr. Penney had converted much of the farm into bluegrass pasture for cattle. Nearly every day he made a trip to the farm to look after the cattle and to inspect the fences. Today he planned to take Mittie and Elie with him to help with his work.

"May I go to the farm with you?" begged Jimmy when Mr. Penney was ready to start.

"Yes," replied Mr. Penney. "Wait until Mittie and Elie climb in. Then you can climb in."

Soon all the children were seated in the cart and Mr. Penney drove away. "Father, what do you plan to let Jimmy do at the farm today?" asked Elie on the way to the country. "He's too little to do regular work on the farm."

"Of course he is," replied Mr. Penney, "but today we're just going on an inspection trip to the farm."

"What's an 'in-spec-tion' trip?" asked Jimmy, slowly repeating the new word.

"Well, we're going to check the cattle to see that they are all right," replied Mr. Penney. "We'll want to see how both the big cattle and the calves are getting along. Mostly, however, we're going to check the fences to see that they are in good shape."

"With nearly four hundred acres in Bluegrass Farm, and the farm broken up into pastures and fields for growing crops, there are many fences to look after," added Elie.

"We'll need to check all the fences around the pastures very carefully," continued Mr. Penney. "Right now with so many head of cattle on the farm and some of them about ready for market, we can't take any chances. If the fences are down or weakened in places, some of the cattle might get out and wander off."

Mr. Penney and the children kept talking as the little cart bounced along the dirt road the two and a half miles to the farm. Jimmy had been born on the farm, and sometimes he wished that the family still lived there. He liked the wide open spaces on the farm.

"Whoa, Ned," Mr. Penney called when they came to the farm. "Let's go to the barns first."

The horse gently jogged along a lane that led to the big barn on the farm. When the cart stopped rolling, the three children immediately jumped out. They decided to go on foot to the spot where they would begin their work for the day. Elie led the way on the run, but Mittie, not to be outdone, jogged along, too. They ran slowly, however, to let Jimmy with his short legs keep up with them.

Jimmy had often come to the farm on short trips, but he didn't remember anybody ever inspecting fences on the farm. Just what would they do to inspect fences, he wondered. Before long he would know.

When Mr. Penney joined the children, he began to explain the work to be done. "Take hold of the strands of barbwire and shake them to make sure they are fastened firmly to the wooden posts. Check the posts to see that they are standing straight. Push them to make sure they are set firmly in the ground or haven't rotted or broken off. Give special attention to the big posts in the corners of the fields. Make

16

sure they are anchored firmly to keep the long strands of barbwire tight."

Elie held out two pairs of heavy gloves that he had brought from the cart. "Let's divide the work," he said. "I'll check the barbwire, which is the most disagreeable job." Next he turned to Mittie. "Here, Mittie, are some gloves for you. Give each post a shove to see whether it seems to be solidly in the ground."

"Jimmy, you may be a weed-hunter," put in Mr. Penney.

"Weed-hunter?" Jimmy asked.

"Yes," explained Mr. Penney. "In order to have good bluegrass pasture, we have to be sure that no weeds are growing in the fields. As we walk along the fences, look carefully for thistles and other kinds of weeds. Then tell me when you find one. Do you understand?"

"Oh, sure," replied Jimmy as he started along a fence to look for weeds.

"Shake, shake, shake," called Elie as he grasped a strand of barbwire on the fence.

"Push, push, push," laughed Mittie as she pushed on a wooden fencepost.

"Hunt, hunt, hunt," called Jimmy, entering into the spirit of the group. Gleefully he stood pointing toward several thistles along the edge of the field.

Mr. Penney took a big Barlow knife from his pocket and opened it to use the larger blade of the two. Then he dug out the thistles, roots and all. "We need something to put all these thistles in," he said. "I don't want them to lie here and take root again. Which one of you will run to the barn to get a gunny sack to put the weeds in? Then we'll save the weeds to form a compost for our garden."

"I'll go," volunteered Jimmy. Before the older children could answer, he started to run to the barn. Soon he came back and proudly handed a big gunny sack to his father. "Here it is, Father," he said.

"You may be small for your age, but you surely can run fast," laughed Elie.

"Stop calling me 'small,' " Jimmy complained. "I'll bet I'm as big as you were when you were almost five. I'll be five in September."

Jimmy turned to his father. "Father, how big was Elie when he was almost five years old?" He stood with his back to the fence with three strands of barbwire stretched from post to post. "See, I'm almost as tall as the fence."

"Now, boys, we want no arguments," interrupted Mr. Penney. "Size doesn't mean anything. Each of you has a job to do, and I am sure each of you can do your job well."

Elie whispered to Jimmy. "We might as well not argue. It sounds as if Father is going to give us a Sunday sermon on Wednesday." He chuckled at his own idea.

Jimmy giggled, too, because his father had started talking in the same tone of voice that he used in preaching sermons on Sunday. Every Sunday Mr. Penney drove twelve miles from Hamilton to preach at Log Creek Primitive Baptist Church. Often it seemed to the boys that he quoted Bible lessons all week long.

As Mr. Penney and the children worked along the fences, they stopped from time to time to look at nearby cattle. "Let's count them to see whether any are missing," said Mr. Penney. "Always there is danger that some have been stolen. Also, we must watch for cattle that may be sick or injured, especially calves. Then before we go home, we must make sure the cattle have plenty of water and salt."

Elie and Mittie kept inspecting the fences and Jimmy kept pointing out thistles and other weeds for Mr. Penney to cut out with his knife. Jimmy dragged the gunny sack from one weed to another. The nearer it became filled, the harder he found it to handle.

At first Jimmy thought that working on the farm was a great adventure. As the Missouri sun rose higher and higher in the clear blue sky, however, he became hot and tired. Then he decided that farming was hard work.

At Log Creek Church

ONE SUNDAY morning in late fall, Mr. Penney prepared to drive to the Log Creek Primitive Baptist Church for his Sunday preaching services. "May I go with you next Sunday?" asked Jimmy as he came out to help his father hitch the horse to the buggy.

"Well, as you know, your mother often goes with me when the weather is good," replied Mr. Penney. "Besides you get to hear me preach from time to time here at home, but if you work hard this week maybe I'll let you go with me next Sunday."

Every Sunday Jimmy and his brothers and sisters attended Sunday School and church services at the Hamilton Baptist Church. Always, however, he was eager to go with his father to attend services in the Log Creek Primitive Baptist Church. He wanted to see just where his father went to preach.

When the next Sunday morning rolled around, his mother awakened him by whispering softly, "Jimmy, get up for breakfast. Your father says you may go with him today."

"What—where——" mumbled Jimmy as he tried to think what was going on. His mother did not tarry to answer him but hurried back downstairs to finish getting breakfast.

Finally he awakened enough to realize what was happening. His father was going to take him to the Log Creek Church to reward him for working hard during the week. He had spent many hours preparing the family garden for winter. He had pulled the corn stalks from the rows of corn and cleared away all the dead bean and pea vines left from the summer.

"Yes, today I, James Cash Penney, get to go with my father, the Reverend James Cash Penney," he thought as he hurried into his best clothes. "I don't get to spend much time with Father alone. This trip is going to be great."

"My, how good you look all dressed up!" exclaimed his mother when he entered the kitchen. "I'm glad it's a clear day so you can go, but it is cold this morning. I have some bricks warming on the stove to place at your feet. Also I have a big heavy quilt warming in front of the stove to place over your lap."

Jimmy grinned. He had watched the weather all week. If the weather had become bad, he couldn't have gone, because his father would have ridden alone on horseback.

"Hurry to eat your hot cakes and bacon so we can get started," said Mr. Penney, rising from the table. "While you finish eating, I'll go on out to hitch the horse to the buggy."

After Jimmy finished his breakfast, he hurried outside and climbed into the buggy. His mother put the bricks under his feet and tucked the warm quilt around him. A few minutes later his father climbed in beside him and snapped the reins on the horse's back. Then they started on the long ride to the church.

For a while they rode along silently. Jimmy was careful not to disturb Mr. Penney's thoughts. Often he had heard his mother say that his father always used the time going to the church to think of what he wanted to say.

Jimmy snuggled his arms tightly against his body and studied the pieces in the quilt. These pieces were of many different sizes and shapes. They had been put together to form what was known as a crazy-quilt pattern.

Weeks before Jimmy had watched his mother

make this quilt. As he looked at the various pieces, he tried to remember where she had obtained them. Readily he recognized pieces which she had taken from his old Sunday suit that had been his father's suit. First she had cut the suit down for Elie, and next she had made it smaller for him. Finally when the elbows had become thin, she had cut out the best parts for making quilts. Some of them she had used in making this quilt, and other parts she would use in making other quilts.

"How far is it to Log Creek Church?" Jimmy finally asked, breaking the silence.

Mr. Penney was happy to begin talking with his son. He had appreciated Jimmy's remaining silent so he could think of his sermon. "The church is twelve miles from our place in Hamilton," he said. "It takes about two hours to make the trip when the weather is good. In bad weather it takes a little longer."

"Do you like preaching every Sunday and working on the farm all week?" asked Jimmy.

"That's an interesting question, but somehow I never stopped to think about it," replied Mr. Penney. "When I graduated from Pleasant Ridge College, I was thankful to have a good education, something many people lack an opportunity to obtain these days. Then I decided to use my education for the Lord."

"Mother says you aren't paid any money for preaching twice every Sunday," said Jimmy. "That doesn't seem right to me."

A slow grin spread over Mr. Penney's face. "Well, it's true that I don't get paid any money for preaching," he explained, "but I am paid in other ways. My pay comes from watching people listen closely to the lessons that I explain from the Bible. If I can bring them a few good thoughts to help them through the week, then I have done a good deed."

Mr. Penney paused in thought for a moment. "Some churches are beginning to pay preachers," he added. "Doubtless the time will come when preachers will be paid not only to preach sermons on Sunday but to minister to their congregations throughout the week. I'd like nothing better than to give up farming and devote all my time to helping people."

"Sometimes I think I'd like to be a preacher," said Jimmy. "I enjoy reading and studying the Bible, and I've learned many Bible verses. Besides, I always say my prayers."

"Maybe being a preacher will be your calling in life," agreed Mr. Penney. "One thing is sure, no matter what you become, you always should think of others and their needs. I know that the people of Log Creek need a preacher. I have wanted to serve them, not only for their good but for mine, too. There is something a little selfish about being unselfish."

Jimmy did not answer but just sat thinking for a minute. For a five-year-old boy this statement was a bit too much to understand. He clearly grasped the meaning, however, of what his father said about thinking of others and their needs. Already he had been taught to understand the Golden Rule: "Do unto others as you would have them do unto you."

A half hour later Mr. Penney and Jimmy pulled up at the little Log Creek Primitive Baptist Church. Already a row of horses and buggies was drawn up to the hitching posts in front of the church. A few horses were hitched to nearby trees in the church yard.

"Hurry, Jimmy," called Mr. Penney. "It's almost time to start the services."

Jimmy jumped down and followed his father up the steps into the church. There was only one small room inside with a raised platform in front. The pews consisted merely of long stiff benches. Most of the pews were filled with people, ready for the services to start.

Mr. Penney went directly to the platform, and Jimmy sat in a front pew where he could listen carefully to the services. He was especially proud of the way in which his father spoke. He did not rant and rave at the people as some preachers did. Besides, he seemed to mean exactly what he said as he spoke.

As soon as the services ended, there was a noisy hum of voices. A leader in the church announced in a loud voice, "Since it is cold outside today, we'll eat our dinner inside the church. We'll need to shove the pews to one side and set up a long table in the center of the room. Will the menfolks please proceed with the heavy work so that the womenfolks can spread out the food? You boys may help to move the pews."

"Oh, boy!" thought Jimmy. "This is going to be the best part of the service."

30

Some of the children gathered around Jimmy and began to talk with him, eager to get acquainted with the preacher's son. Then they began to help shove the pews to one side.

The men got wooden sawhorses and boards from the rear of the church. They placed the boards on the sawhorses to form a long table. In the meantime the women and children carried in baskets of food from the buggies.

As soon as the long table was ready, the women spread big white tablecloths over the boards. At one end of the table they placed big platters of chicken and ham. Near the middle they put large bowls of green beans, sauerkraut, sweet potatoes, potato salad, deviled eggs, cucumber pickles, beet pickles, and cole slaw. At the other end they set out rich chocolate cakes, angel food cakes, apple pies, cherry pies, gooseberry pies, and walnut pies.

"Jimmy," Mr. Penny called to his son when

it was time to eat, "come to stand here with me while we ask the blessing of the Lord on this most bounteous meal."

Jimmy stood proudly beside his father as Mr. Penney said grace. After his prayer, the members one by one walked along the table and filled their plates high with food. Then they sat down here and there to eat and to talk about farming and the weather.

The children finished quickly and ran outside to play Blind Man's Buff. The Primitive Baptists believed in reserving the Sabbath for worship but did not deny their children the privilege of playing on Sunday.

After everyone had finished eating, the women gathered up their dirty dishes and placed them in baskets to take home. The men carried the long boards and wooden sawhorses to the rear of the room, and the boys returned all the pews to their proper places.

One of the elders of the church went to the door and announced, "Come on in. It's time for the afternoon services to begin."

Once more the children sat close to their parents and attempted to listen, but found the services too difficult for them to understand. During the morning services they had managed to sit fairly still and partly listen, but by now they were fidgety and uneasy.

Feet scuffed against the floor as they moved aimlessly here and there. Toes kicked the seats in front with a continuous *thud, thud,* and fingers drummed constantly on the stiff wooden benches. Finally heads nodded from failure to understand the preaching that was intended only for adults. Jimmy was proud of his father's preaching, but he had a hard time to keep from nodding along with many others.

It was late afternoon before the last "Amen" was sounded and Jimmy bade good-by to his new friends. Then he and Mr. Penney climbed into their buggy and started back to town. "You got a little sleepy this afternoon, didn't you?" chuckled Mr. Penney.

"I'm sorry, Father," Jimmy confessed sheepishly. "This morning I heard everything you said, even though I didn't always understand what you meant. This afternoon I tried to listen to everything, too, but finally I sort of dozed off a little."

"Don't worry about it, son," Mr. Penney said gently. "All children should listen to services with their parents to learn as much as possible about the Bible. Even though they don't always understand exactly what the preacher says, maybe someday his words will come back to them with special meaning."

Jimmy nodded thoughtfully. "You certainly made it easy to listen this morning."

Mr. Penney spoke slowly. "Each Sunday at

home you go to the Hamilton Baptist Church, which has a Sunday school in addition to preaching services. Probably this church is doing a better job of teaching young people than the Log Creek Primitive Baptist Church. Do you enjoy going to Sunday school?"

"I surely do," replied Jimmy. "We study Bible stories and always seem to understand the lessons that we are supposed to get from the stories. Why don't you have a Sunday school at the Log Creek Primitive Baptist Church?"

"Different churches have been formed because different people prefer different ways to worship," explained Mr. Penney. "Primitive, or Old School, Baptists, as some folks call them, believe that children should hear only the same things that grown-ups hear. They are afraid that separate services might corrupt young people."

"Corrupt?" asked Jimmy, shaking his head. "What does that mean?"

"Well, probably that's too big a word and too strong a word," said Mr. Penney. "Anyway, they believe that Sunday schools shouldn't be held. I never have discussed the question at the Log Creek Church. One of these days when we have a good debate going, I plan to propose starting a Sunday school there."

As father and son continued the ride, the shadows became longer and longer and the air became cooler and cooler. Jimmy snuggled under the big quilt to keep warm, and his head slumped over on his father's shoulder. Thus the twelve miles which Mr. Penney had traveled in the service of the Lord slowly came to an end.

"Good Morning, Mrs. Maple"

MRS. PENNEY stopped suddenly as she was hanging up clothes to dry on the line. She thought she heard someone crying in front of the house and wondered who it could be.

She hurried around the house. There she found Jimmy sobbing loudly on the front steps. "James Cash Penney, what are you doing back home?" she called. "Less than an hour ago you left here to attend your first day of school. When you left, you were one of the happiest boys I ever saw."

At first Mrs. Penney was inclined to be angry, but when she saw how hard Jimmy was crying, she stopped scolding him. She sat down beside him, wiped his face with the end of her apron, and tried to comfort him. "There, there," she said, patting him on the shoulder. "Let me wipe your tears away. Now tell me what happened."

Jimmy looked up. "I don't—know—what—happened," he said.

"But that doesn't make sense," sighed Mrs. Penney. "Why did you come back home?"

"I—I—I had a fight," wailed Jimmy.

"You had a fight!" exclaimed Mrs. Penney. "How in the world could you have a fight in such a short time? Why, you haven't been gone from home long enough to get into a fight. Tell me what happened."

Jimmy tried to explain. "Well, I was running hard to get to school, and I guess I didn't watch where I was going. When I turned around to call to one of the McDonald boys, I hit my head smack-dab into some bigger boy's stomach. I don't even know who the boy was, but all of a sudden he hit me."

Jimmy paused, and Mrs. Penney patted his shoulder. "Then what happened?" she asked.

"Well, without thinking I turned around and hit him back," replied Jimmy. "Next he was going to hit me, but a big boy stepped between us and made us stop fighting. He said we would be whipped because children aren't allowed to fight at school. So I just came running back home as fast as I could."

"Oh, Jimmy," moaned Mrs. Penney, "what a way to start your first day at school! Why, you haven't even been in the building yet."

"There wasn't any use of getting a whipping at school and one here, too," continued Jimmy. "You always said that if any of us gets tanned at school we would get tanned at home, too. So I hurried home before I got spanked."

40

Mrs. Penney now had a hard time to keep from laughing at Jimmy's reasoning. She accepted the situation with the understanding heart of a fond mother. She realized that there was no need for punishment.

"All right, young man," she said. "I realize your problem, but don't worry. The teacher probably wouldn't have whipped you because the fight started over an accident. Get your face washed so you can go back to school, and this time I'll go with you. While you're cleaning your face, I'll get one of the neighbors to come to stay with Mattie."

Jimmy went meekly into the kitchen and poured some water into a washpan. Slowly he rubbed his face with a moistened washcloth and dried it with a towel. Soon his mother returned with a neighbor woman to stay with Mattie. "Now you look much better," she said. "Put your cap on straight, and let's go."

Jimmy would have liked to argue about going, but he knew that arguing would be useless. He and his mother walked along silently for a while. Then Mrs. Penney thought of a plan to take his mind off his troubles. "Do you remember what a boy does when he meets a lady walking along the street?" she asked.

"Sure," replied Jimmy. "He tips his cap."

Mrs. Penney believed a growing boy or girl needed to learn gracious manners. She rarely lost a chance to make games of teaching manners. This trip to school was no exception.

"All right, let's play a game on the way to school," she suggested with a slight twinkle in her eye. "Whenever we come to a big tree, you pretend it is a lady. Then tip your cap and speak politely."

At once Jimmy forgot all about his trouble and entered into the spirit of the game. "All right," he said. "Let me practice. Here is a

42

maple tree, which I'll speak to first. Good morning, Mrs. Maple, how are you today?" He lifted
the bill of his cap slightly as he spoke.

"That was very good," said Mrs. Penney to
compliment him. "Now try another step in

practicing good manners. This time when you tip your cap, give your head a little nod."

Soon they came to another maple tree. "Good morning, Mrs. Maple," said Jimmy, lifting the bill of his cap. At the same time he gave his head a slight nod.

"Very good, Jimmy," said Mrs. Penney in an encouraging tone of voice.

As they walked on Jimmy kept speaking to maple trees, tipping his cap and nodding his head. Finally he laughingly said, "We surely meet many Mrs. Maples along the way."

Mrs. Penney was determined to keep him from thinking about going back to school. At last she said, "Last year you heard Elie study his geography lessons at home. Let's see whether you remember some of the things he learned. What is the name of the county where we live?"

"That's easy," replied Jimmy quickly. "We live in Caldwell County. The first house ever built in Hamilton was put up in 1855 by Albert G. Davis. It's the big two-story house a couple of blocks from the railroad."

"You not only remembered some of Elie's geography lessons but some of your father's stories about local history," said Mrs. Penney. "I'm surprised that you remember so much."

"I learned, too, that people here used to hold church services in the old depot and that my grandfather Eli Penney was one of the first preachers here," added Jimmy. "Good morning, Mrs. Maple," he said, interrupting his story to tip his cap and nod his head.

A few minutes later they reached the big square brick school building. As they came near, Jimmy walked a little more slowly. He didn't object to entering the building, however, because his mother expected him to go to school. He had no other choice. Already he knew that his parents believed in strict discipline.

Inside the building Mrs. Penney led the way to the primary room with Jimmy following. "Good morning, Mrs. Penney," said the first-grade teacher pleasantly. "I'm glad to see you. I have been wondering about Jimmy because he didn't come this morning."

Jimmy felt relieved when the teacher didn't say anything about his fight. "Maybe she didn't even hear about it," he thought. "Anyhow, I didn't mean to have one. I just accidentally bumped the big boy and he hit me. Then naturally I hit him back before I even knew what I was doing."

Jimmy listened as his mother continued to talk with the teacher. "Well," said Mrs. Penney, "Jimmy started to come this morning, but he had to return home. Now I have come with him to help him enroll as a beginner. He is only five years old at present, but he will be six on the sixteenth of September."

"Thank you," said the teacher. "Now that you have come, I'll ask you the questions for filling in his enrollment record. Then he can join the class and get started with studying his arithmetic lesson." She paused to call a boy near the front of the room. "John, will you get Jimmy an arithmetic book?"

John took Jimmy to a seat and handed him a small book with a reddish-brown cover. On the front cover of the book was a picture of a lady holding big number cards before a little boy and girl. The title of the book, which was printed in large letters above the picture, was *Ray's Arithmetic, First Book*. On the title page of the book there was a subtitle, *Primary Lessons and Tables in Arithmetic for Young Learners*. This book was used by little boys and girls in many schools in the United States to learn their first lessons in arithmetic.

John showed Jimmy what lesson to study in

the book. "The teacher says this lesson will teach us how to count in words," he explained. "I'll bet you already know how to say your numbers up to ten, don't you?"

"Sure I do," said Jimmy, rattling off, "One-two-three-four-five-six-seven-eight-nine-ten."

"Notice the pictures of balls," said John, pointing toward the center of the page. "At the right beside the pictures of balls, there are words and numbers. Now in the first line at the top of the page, there is a picture of one ball and across from this ball at the right there is a word and beside the word there is a number. You can guess what the word and number are because there is only one ball."

"Of course," said Jimmy. "The word says 'one' and the number says 'one.' "

"You're right," said John.

Jimmy smiled. "Now I am ready to read by myself," he said. "The next line has two balls, so the word is 'two' and the number is 'two.' This is going to be easy, if all I need to do is count the balls and read the words and numbers beside them."

He counted the balls and read the lines over and over to himself, "One ball—o-n-e—one. One, two balls—t-w-o—two. One, two, three balls— t-h-r-e-e—three." He found reading the words especially easy, because he already knew all the letters in the alphabet, even the small letters.

Soon he was able to read all the words and numbers without counting the balls. He was so busy studying that he didn't even notice when his mother slipped away.

Later in the day Jimmy had a lesson in a *McGuffey First Reader* and a lesson in a *Webster Blue-Back Speller*. By the end of the day he had decided that he liked studying and might enjoy coming to school after all.

Buttering the Churn

ONE AFTERNOON Jimmy was rushing home from school. Suddenly he heard Jim McDonald calling to him, "Hey, Jimmy, can you come over to play ball with us this afternoon?"

"I think so, but first I'll have to go home to ask my mother," replied Jimmy. "And I'll have to finish my left-over chores."

"Well, hurry," called Jim. "We may not have enough players without you."

Jimmy dashed on. All the way home he tried to think of what chores he might have to do. Both his parents insisted on his doing his chores regularly and on time.

50

He thought first about things that he might need to do in his room. He had made his bed and picked up his dirty clothes. He had helped his mother with the dishes at noon and put them in their proper places on the pantry shelves.

When he reached home, he rushed into the kitchen where his mother was busy mending family clothes. "Mother," he said eagerly, "I have finished doing my chores now until after suppertime. May I go play ball for a while with some of the boys, please?"

His mother looked at him in surprise. "Why, Jimmy, this is the afternoon for you to churn," she replied. "I have saved enough cream to make a nice batch of butter."

Jimmy had completely forgotten about the churning. He was disappointed, but he didn't try to argue. "Maybe if I hurry with the churning, I can still go to play ball for a while before dark," he said. "May I please, Mother?"

"Of course, if you still want to go," replied Mrs. Penney. "While you are churning I'll go to take care of little Pearl. She seems to be waking from a nap."

Little Pearl now was nearly one and one half years old. Her birth had helped the Penneys overcome great grief in the family. Mollie had died in January and Mattie in March before Pearl had been born in April, 1882.

Jimmy went to the pantry and brought out the big crockery churn. Usually he churned in the kitchen, but today he decided to churn outside on the back porch. He brought out a crock of cream and poured it into the churn.

Mrs. Penney had filled the crock with cream which she had saved. Each day she put fresh warm milk into crocks to let it cool overnight. During the night a thick layer of cream formed on the milk, which she skimmed off with a blade-like dipper.

After Jimmy finished pouring the thick yellow cream into the churn, he put the dasher down into the churn with its long handle sticking upward. Then he put the hole in the churn lid on the handle and slid the lid down firmly onto the top of the churn.

Slowly he began the tedious job of moving the dasher up and down, up and down, up and down. Usually he didn't mind this job very much because he could always practice his multiplication tables or his spelling as he worked. Today he decided to practice saying his fours. "Four times one is four. Four times two is eight. Four times three is——"

Jimmy kept on churning, but somehow the cream in the churn didn't thicken as usual. It never occurred to him that the warm outside air was making the cream too warm for particles of butter to form. "By the time I get to the elevens, I usually see butter on the lid," he thought.

"Now of all days for something like this to happen when I want to go play ball for a while! I think I'll go inside to get a few cookies to eat while I finish churning."

He left the churn standing in the warm sunshine, went inside, and pulled several fat ginger snaps from a well-filled cookie jar. Then, while he was near, he decided to look at the butter dish to see how much butter was left from the last batch which he had churned. "Why, there is plenty of butter here for our supper and then some," he thought. "We don't need butter as much as I thought we did."

He went back to the porch and began moving the dasher up and down again. He ate the cookies slowly, and hoped that the butter would soon begin to form, but nothing happened. At last he realized that the cream had become too warm for particles of butter to collect.

"Now what am I going to do?" he wondered.

54

"I shouldn't have brought the churn to the back porch. No butter will form now until the cream cools off. I might as well be out there playing ball for all the good my churning is doing. I know what I'll do. I'll put the churn in the pantry so the cream will cool and I can finish churning this evening. In the meantime I'll get some butter out of the pantry and smear it on the lid of the churn around the handle. Then Mother will think that the butter has formed in the churn and that I have finished my work."

He rushed to the pantry, scooped up a little butter with his fingers, and smeared it on the lid of the churn around the handle. Moments later he called to his mother, "I've put the churn in the pantry to cool, and I'm leaving now to play ball. I'll take out the butter and clean the churn after I get back."

Later when Mrs. Penney was preparing supper, she noticed bits of butter on the lid and assumed that Jimmy had finished churning. Finally, when she had a few minutes to spare, she decided to help him by taking the butter from the churn. Then she was shocked when she removed the lid to find that the churn still contained only thick yellow cream.

She stared down at the cream and could scarcely believe that Jimmy had deceived her. Obviously he had smeared butter on the top of the churn to make her think that he had finished his work. Then she wondered whether her strict discipline in dealing with him led him to deceive her. At any rate she decided that he should be punished for deceiving her.

This willful act on Jimmy's part led him to realize that honesty was the best policy. After he returned home, he was punished both with a hickory stick and a stern lecture.

Holes in
the Soles

"DON'T LEAVE that pan standing there on the cabinet, Jimmy," said Mrs. Penney. "You always should put the pots and pans away just as neatly as you put the dishes away."

Jimmy hastily put the pan away. "Sure I know better," he explained, "but I was in a hurry to begin studying words in my spelling book. We are going to have a spelling bee at school tomorrow, and I want to make a good showing. Spelling is my favorite subject at school."

"After I finish ironing, I'll pronounce the words for you," said Mittie as she moved the iron slowly over a towel on the ironing board.

58

"Spelling words that way will be the best way to get ready for the spelling bee."

"Thank you, Mittie," said Jimmy. "I'll study by myself until you are ready."

Jimmy took his little *Blue-Black Speller* as everyone called the book, and sat down to study. The real title of the book was *Elementary Spelling Book* by Noah Webster. There were additional words on the title page which read, "Being an improvement on 'The American Spelling Book,' the cheapest, the best and the most extensively used spelling book published."

First Jimmy decided to study Lesson No. 75, "Words of Three Syllables, Accented on the Second." He noted that the words were arranged in columns with the pronunciation marked and the syllables divided. Then he started to study each word just as he would spell it if he were called upon to spell it in the spelling bee the next day. He spelled and pronounced each syllable, then pronounced it with the preceding syllable or syllables, as "Arrival, a-r, ar, r-i, ri, arri, v-a-l, val, arrival."

After Jimmy had gone through the words *approval, coeval, refusal, reprisal, perusal, decretal, recital, requital, primeval,* he heard his father calling him. "I'm sorry to interrupt you while you are studying, but I have an important matter to discuss with you," he said.

"I'm glad to stop for a while," replied Jimmy. "I may need you to help me figure out what some of these three-syllable words mean. Some of the harder ones are included in sentences at the end of the lesson. For instance, I don't remember ever having heard anyone use the word 'coeval,' but it's included in the speller. Then it is used in a sentence below and seems to mean 'of the same age.' "

"Yes, Jimmy, some of those three-syllable words are hard," said Mr. Penney, "but you can master them. Your mother and I want you to do well in school. And now that you are eight years old you are old enough to assume another responsibility. From now on you will be expected to buy your own clothes."

"Buy my own clothes!" exclaimed Jimmy, stunned by this abrupt announcement from his father. He could scarcely believe that Mr. Penney meant what he said.

"Yes, buy your own clothes," repeated Mr. Penney. "You are now old enough to earn enough money to provide yourself with whatever new clothes you need. Some of your clothes are made from old clothes that Elie and I have worn. Of course, you won't have to pay for any of your handed-down clothes."

Mr. Penney paused, and Jimmy attempted to ask a question. "You always have bought new shoes for us children. Each of my shoes has a big hole in the sole. I need a new pair of shoes right now. Will you buy me one more pair? Then while I wear out the new pair, I will save money to buy the next pair."

Mr. Penney didn't hesitate in answering his son's plea. "Your responsibility starts now," he said, "and you'll have to figure out some way to earn money to buy the new shoes yourself. It's easier to work to earn money when you have a real need and goal."

"Please, just one more pair?" begged Jimmy.

"No, I have tried to help each of you children to learn to be self-reliant," replied Mr. Penney. "Your brother Elie began to earn money to buy his own clothes a long time ago. I am sure you will find a way to buy yours."

Without further comment, Mr. Penney left Jimmy staring blankly at the three-syllable words in his spelling book. Jimmy's thoughts were far from studying the words before him. How could he solve this new and unexpected problem?

Moments later he decided to appeal to his mother. "Mother," he said in a pleading voice, "did you know that Father is going to make me earn money to buy my own clothes? Will you pay me for some of the chores that I do here at home, so that I may earn money? I make my bed, wash or dry the dishes, milk the cow, churn to make butter, and plow the fields. I could be paid for doing some of these things."

"Yes, you do all those things willingly and well, but they are merely things that you are supposed to do as a member of the family. We all share our work as well as our food and home. I'll make things for you from time to time when I have any old clothes that are good enough. But you will have to find ways of earning money to buy other things you need."

"Father says that earning money will help me to become 'self-reliant,'" protested Jimmy, "but I sure don't know how I can start being self-

64

reliant so suddenly. I may have to go bare-footed before I can earn enough money to buy a new pair of shoes."

"Now don't get upset, Jimmy," said his mother reassuringly. "I am sure that you will find a way somehow. Go on to bed and see what you can think of tomorrow."

Jimmy gave his mother a quick good-night kiss. He picked up his speller and stacked it neatly with his other schoolbooks, ready to be carried to school the next day.

Slowly he went up the steps to his room. The moon, shining through the window, made enough light for him to see to get ready for bed. Calmly he unbuttoned each button of his clothes. Then he carefully laid his clothes on the chair beside his bed.

Finally he sat down on the edge of his bed to think. Slowly he picked up his shoes and held them upside down. He stared at the hole in the sole of his left shoe. He stared at the hole in the sole of his right shoe.

There was no anger in his thoughts, only quiet fear. Ever since he could remember he had been willing to do the tasks at home which had been assigned to him. Always, except when he had left the churning undone, he had tried to do his chores promptly and well. He had been proud of doing his share of the work for the family.

Now he faced a problem which seemed to have no solution. There was no way for him to earn money for shoes by the time he needed them. In fact, he needed them right now.

After he crawled into bed, he started to cry, but he didn't want anybody to know that he was crying. His father and mother never seemed to complain when they had troubles. Even when their youngest child, five-month-old Lele Ervin, had died recently, they had depended on prayers rather than tears to bring relief.

66

"I just can't do it," Jimmy thought as he lay listening to the noises of night outside. Soon, however, his feelings of defeat began to give way to the spirit of determination that his father knew he possessed. If others had succeeded, he could succeed, too.

All through the night, he tossed and turned, but with each toss and turn he came up with another idea. Already he was beginning to think of different things that he might do for other people to earn money. The next few weeks and months would reveal how successful he would be. At least, he now was willing to try!

Nails and Nickels

"WELL, FIRST I'll try to get a job at the black-smith shop," Jimmy thought the next morning as he pulled on his worn-out shoes. Within a few weeks his school year would be finished. Surely during the summer he could find some sort of work to do.

Somehow the idea of having to buy his own clothes didn't seem nearly as bad now as it had the night before. During his long wakeful hours in the night, he had thought of several persons around town whom he might ask for jobs. One was his friend Mr. Thomas, the blacksmith, whom he hoped to see on his way to school.

Hurriedly he made his bed before he went downstairs. Next he went out to the barn to milk the family cow. While he was milking, he planned exactly what he would say when he stopped to ask for a job.

At the breakfast table Mr. Penney read from the Bible and offered a morning prayer. Jimmy tried to listen, but all the while he was thinking of his visit to the blacksmith shop.

For breakfast Mrs. Penney placed a big platter of bacon with hot biscuits and molasses on the table. Jimmy ate his share rapidly and hoped the others would eat rapidly too, so he could start to help with the dishes. After he finished eating, he had to sit quietly at the table and wait for the others to finish.

As he waited, he swung his feet back and forth impatiently. He watched closely until all the others had consumed their food. Then in order to get started with his work, he said politely to his mother, "If you have finished, I'll carry your dishes from the table."

"Thank you, Jimmy, that will be fine," said Mrs. Penney. Then Mr. Penney, Mittie, Elie, and even little Pearl handed Jimmy their plates, milk glasses, knives, forks, and spoons.

Everybody laughed at the new servant in the family. "We usually don't have anybody so eager to work that he wants to do everything himself," added Mrs. Penney.

Jimmy smiled but didn't explain why he was in such a hurry. After he finished doing the dishes, he rushed to the blacksmith shop to talk with Mr. Thomas. When he entered the door, he found Mr. Thomas standing before a blazing fire in the forge. He was holding a piece of iron in the fire with his tongs to make it red-hot for hammering.

Jimmy always liked to watch Mr. Thomas work, but this morning there was no time for watching. He had come for a different purpose and had no time to waste. "Mr. Thomas," he said, "I've noticed when I stop here after school that your floor always is littered with old nails. Who picks up all those nails for you?"

"Why, I pick them up myself," replied Mr. Thomas, paying little attention to Jimmy's question. He was accustomed to having children stand about, watching and asking questions.

"Well, sir, I should like a job of picking up the nails," said Jimmy. "I'll come by and pick them up every afternoon, if you'll pay me."

"If I'll pay you!" exclaimed Mr. Thomas in surprise. "I thought boys always were glad to do odd jobs just for the privilege of getting to watch me work."

"My father has just told me that I have to earn money to buy my own clothes," explained Jimmy. "So I thought you might need someone to pick up your old nails from the floor."

"I'll be glad to save the time and my back in picking up the nails, but I can't pay you very much," said Mr. Thomas. "The most I can pay will be a penny a day."

Jimmy smiled. "I'll agree to a penny a day," he said. "Thank you, Mr. Thomas. Now I have to hurry on or I'll be late for school. I'll see you this afternoon."

Lightheartedly he ran on to school. Already he had a job to begin to earn money. A penny a day for picking up old nails wouldn't buy many clothes, but at least he had a job. At school he found it very hard to keep his mind on his books or what the teacher was saying. Instead, he kept trying to think of other jobs he might get to earn money.

That afternoon at the blacksmith shop, Jimmy demonstrated that he was a careful and useful worker. When he stopped working, he had picked up every nail in sight. "You've done a very good job," said Mr. Thomas. "If you do as good a job every afternoon, I'll be glad to pay you. Here is your penny for today."

Jimmy was happy as he left the blacksmith shop. He proudly clutched the penny in his hand all the way home. Then he took it directly to his room and put it in a box before starting his evening chores.

On the remaining spring days Jimmy tried other ways to earn money. He asked different neighbors whether they needed anyone to run errands. "I'll run short errands for five cents and long errands for ten cents," he said.

He made the rounds of the neighborhood every day. Every time he ran an errand, he added the money to his savings.

When late spring came, he thought of the possibility of cutting grass on some of the neighbors' yards, but he had no tools for the purpose. One night he said to Mr. Penney, "Father, I would like to offer to cut grass on a few of the neighbors' yards, but I have no scythe and sickle. Do I have to buy some of my own, or may I use yours?"

Mr. Penney had not anticipated this sort of question. "You have taken me by surprise, Jimmy," he said. "I was thinking only of your doing different kinds of work that you could do with your hands and legs."

"Yes, I know," said Jimmy.

"Well, if you can find any work on the neighbors' lawns, you may use my scythe and sickle, but be careful in using them," said Mr. Penney.

"Thank you, Father," said Jimmy.

"Your mother and I are very proud of the way you have started," added Mr. Penney. "We want you to work because we love you and want you to learn to take care of yourself."

Again Jimmy spoke up. "I understand, and I'm very glad," he said.

The next Saturday morning Jimmy set out to find lawns to mow in the neighborhood. Finally Mrs. Brown, who lived nearby, said she would give him twenty-five cents for mowing her lawn. He worked for several hours, cutting the grass with the big scythe. He trimmed carefully along the edges and the walk with the sickle. Finally he took out his knife and dug out all the weeds that were trying to get started.

After he had finished, he went to the door and knocked. "Mrs. Brown," he said, "please come to see whether I have cut the grass just as you wanted me to cut it."

Mrs. Brown came outside and looked all about the yard. "You have done a very good job," she said in a pleased tone of voice.

When she returned to the back porch, she invited Jimmy to come into the house. "Come inside," she said. "You must be warm after working so hard in the hot sun."

Jimmy followed her into the house. Once inside, she continued to speak. "While you have been working on the lawn, I've been baking cookies. Now if you are willing, I would like to pay you for your work with this box of cookies. Certainly they are worth more than the twenty-five cents I agreed to pay you."

"Thank you, Mrs. Brown," said Jimmy in great surprise. "I know your cookies are good, but I can't accept them for pay. My father and mother expect me to work to earn money to buy my own clothes. They don't expect me to buy things to eat or accept food for pay. I cut your grass this morning for money."

Mrs. Brown smiled at Jimmy's long and serious explanation. "That's all right," she said. "I wasn't trying to get out of paying you for your work by offering you some of my cookies. If you really prefer money, I'll gladly pay you. Here is the quarter that I promised you."

"Thank you very much," said Jimmy as he left the house with his scythe and sickle.

One evening late in June, Jimmy sat in his room counting his money. "How much have you earned so far this summer?" asked Elie.

"I have earned an even dollar," replied Jimmy, "and it has taken me a long time to earn this much. The jobs I get around here surely don't pay very much."

"Well, I'm going to give you a chance to make your earnings grow quickly," said Elie.

"How's that?" asked Jimmy excitedly.

"Tomorrow I am supposed to work for Mr. Hamey," explained Elie. "In taking this job, I forgot that I had promised Father to drive the team and wagon to help harvest wheat. How would you like to help Father in my place?"

"How would I like to drive the team and wagon in your place!" exclaimed Jimmy. "Why, of course I would like it, if Father will let me."

"Let's find out," said Elie.

He put his arm around Jimmy's shoulders and the two boys walked side by side to find Mr. Penney. They found him in the living room preparing his sermon for the following Sunday. "Father," interrupted Elie, "I have a big problem, but I think Jimmy can help me solve it."

"Of course I can," piped up Jimmy before Elie could explain what the problem was.

Once more Elie started to talk. "You see, I forgot that I had promised to help you harvest wheat tomorrow, and I promised Mr. Hamey to work for him. Now I wonder whether you'll let Jimmy drive the team and wagon in my place. He is trying hard to earn money, and you planned to pay me for working."

"Yes, an older person usually drives the team and wagon, but I know Jimmy will be careful," agreed Mr. Penney.

"Oh, thank you, Father!" cried Jimmy, rush-

78

ing off to tell his mother about his good fortune. He knew that she would be glad to know that he was going to do a man's work in helping to harvest the wheat.

That night Jimmy went to bed happier than he had been since his father had first told him that he would have to earn money to buy his own clothes. Now for the first time he was going to work with men and do a man's job. He went to sleep thinking of the important work he would do the next day.

Early the next morning at the breakfast table Jimmy listened patiently as his father read several verses from the Bible and offered his morning prayer. After breakfast, he helped his father hitch the horse to the little two-wheeled cart, and he and his father rode off together to the farm. When they arrived, they found several men busy cutting the standing wheat with cradles and tying it into bundles.

Jimmy and his father hitched a team of horses to a wagon and drove to the edge of the wheat field. Then Jimmy waited in the wagon while his father went to help the men who cut and bound the wheat. Nearly all farms in this part of the country still depended on cradles for cutting wheat, but someday Mr. Penney hoped to purchase a new machine called a reaper. This machine was pulled by horses and cut the grain with moving blades. Up to now only one farmer in Caldwell County owned a reaper.

Before long Mr. Penney called to Jimmy to come with the horses and wagon. The men had cut a strip of standing wheat across the field to form an open driveway for the horses and wagon. "Your job is to drive along this strip where the wheat has been cut and stack the bundles of wheat on the wagon as we throw them up to you. Then drive to the barns and help unload the bundles and stack them inside."

The work of cutting the wheat and storing it away in the barn lasted for several days. Jimmy enjoyed every minute and tried to do his part of the work well. He was especially happy on the last day when his father said, "All right, Jimmy, you have finished your work, and now I am ready to pay you. Furthermore, you have done a man's job, not just a little boy's job. Therefore I owe you a total of two dollars and fifty cents for your work."

Jimmy watched proudly as his father counted the money into his outstretched hand. This was the most money he had ever had at one time. At last he could begin to think about how to spend money as well as how to earn money.

Shoes at Last

THE NIGHT AFTER Jimmy finished helping with the harvest, he sat in his room counting his money. At last he had three dollars and fifty cents, enough to buy a new pair of shoes.

For several months the holes in the soles of his shoes had become larger and larger. Repeatedly he had cut pieces of cardboard to put inside the shoes to cover the holes. "From now on I won't have to cut any more pieces of cardboard to put in my shoes," he thought as he laid out his clothes. "Tomorrow I can go to buy a new pair of shoes!"

Early the next morning he set out for a nearby

store. "Good morning, Jimmy," said the clerk, greeting him cheerfully. "What can I do for you today?"

"I want to buy a new pair of shoes," replied Jimmy proudly.

The clerk looked surprised. "Do you want to pick them out alone?" he asked. "Didn't your mother come along to help you select them?"

"No, sir," replied Jimmy. "From now on I am supposed to buy my own clothes. I have worked to earn money to buy this pair of shoes."

Ever since Jimmy had known that he would have to buy his own shoes, he had been checking the prices of shoes shown in store windows. All the shoes that he had seen had been priced at two or three dollars a pair. Now he expected to have to spend nearly all his money for shoes.

Since Jimmy had earned his own money, the clerk assumed that he would want to buy shoes as cheaply as possible. "Here is a good sturdy

84

pair of shoes which you can buy at a reasonable price," he said as he opened a box.

He pulled out two of the ugliest shoes that Jimmy had ever seen. They were clumsy-looking, with big buckles across the instep like the buckles on overshoes or raincoats. A metal latch on one side of each shoe slipped through a metal piece on the opposite side and snapped down to hold the sides together. Underneath the metal buckles there were also laces for holding the shoes together.

At once Jimmy knew that he didn't want this clumsy-looking pair of shoes, but before he could explain the clerk started to talk again. "For a dollar a pair, I think you'll find these shoes about what you want," he said. "Let's slip one of them on for size."

Jimmy was astounded at this low price. "All right," he said. "Let me try one of them on. Did I hear you correctly that the price is only one dollar a pair?" He tried to act as if he were accustomed to buying his own shoes.

Jimmy had a rather small foot and wore smaller shoes than many boys of his age. The first shoe which he tried on was too large. Then he asked the clerk whether he could find a smaller size of the same kind of shoes. "Just wait a minute," said the clerk. "I think I can find a smaller size for you."

He reached up on a high shelf and took down another box. "Here, let's try on one of these," he said.

Already Jimmy had pulled off the first shoe and placed his foot on the fitting stool. The clerk slipped the second shoe on his foot and asked, "How does this one feel?"

"It feels fine," replied Jimmy. "I'll take the smaller pair."

He reached into his pocket and brought out the three dollars and fifty cents which he had brought to the store. Carefully he counted out one dollar and handed it to the clerk. The clerk looked down in surprise to find that Jimmy had so much money. "Have you worked to earn all that money?" he asked.

"Yes, sir," replied Jimmy, "and someday you'll possibly get more of my money. I'll come back to buy other clothing of you, but right now all I need is this pair of shoes. My new shoes aren't very pretty, but they look as if they will wear well. I want to make my earnings go as far as possible."

The clerk was well acquainted with the Penney family. "Well, you'll do all right if you continue to save and spend wisely," he said. "Besides, you have a good name, James Cash Penney, for looking after money. Doubtless you'll make your middle name, Cash, mean something when you become older."

The clerk chuckled at Jimmy's serious expression. Of course he was only joking, but Jimmy resented his associating the name "Cash" with the term "cash" for money. Jimmy's grandfather Rev. Eli Penney had been fond of a preacher named Cash and had named Jimmy's father Cash as a tribute to this friend. Then Jimmy's mother had wanted to name him after her husband. So Jimmy and his father had the same name, James Cash Penney.

When the clerk finished wrapping up the shoes, Jimmy took the package and started for home. Along the way he thought of how ugly the shoes looked, but at the same time he felt that he had made a good deal by buying the shoes so cheaply. Besides, he knew that sturdy shoes made of thick leather would wear better than fancy shoes made of thin leather.

After he reached home, he went directly up to his room, eager to take another look at his shoes. Hurriedly he unwrapped the package and started to examine the shoes carefully. Once more the ugly buckles caught his eyes. "Let's see what use those buckles are anyway," he muttered. "Possibly the shoes would fit my feet just as well without them."

He looked closely and discovered that the buckles were fastened onto the leather with heavy stitching. They could easily be removed and didn't seem to be needed.

At last Jimmy sat down in a chair, pulled off his old shoes, and put on the new shoes. He fastened the laces to see whether the new shoes would fit without fastening the buckles. He tried walking and the buckles kept flapping and catching on things. "Well, the shoes seem to stay on all right, but the buckles are a nuisance," he concluded.

He sat down, took off the shoes, and pulled his knife from his pocket. He knew that his parents would be upset with him if he should ruin a

perfectly good new pair of shoes. At the same time he felt that he would be safe because he still had enough money left from his savings to buy another pair of shoes.

For several minutes he sat trying to decide whether to cut off the buckles or not. He had purchased the shoes in order to save money, but he didn't like their appearance. Certainly he would be justified in taking steps to improve their appearance, if he could.

Finally he picked up one of the shoes and slowly cut off its buckle. Then he picked up the other shoe and slowly cut off its buckle. As far as he could tell, he hadn't damaged the shoes at all. In order to be sure, he decided to try on both shoes again. They seemed to fit well and didn't look nearly as ugly as they had before he removed the buckles. They merely looked as if they would wear well.

At last he had shoes that would last!

An Early Investment

AFTER JIMMY had money left over from buying new shoes, he tried to think of a way to use the money to earn more money. One morning at breakfast he said, "Father, would you care if I use the rest of my money to buy a pig?"

"Buy a pig!" exclaimed Mr. Penney. "Why in the world do you want to buy a pig?"

"Well, I guess I just want to be like you," explained Jimmy. "You raise cattle on your farm to sell after they become big. By raising and selling cattle you make enough money to support our family and to help pay the mortgages on our farm and our home here in town."

92

"That's right," agreed Mr. Penney.

"During the summer you let the cattle graze on the bluegrass on the farm," continued Jimmy. "Then you grow corn on the farm to use as feed for fattening the cattle in the fall and winter. Sometimes you have to buy corn because you don't grow as much as you need."

"Again you're right," said Mr. Penney, amused by Jimmy's seriousness.

"Well, ever since you told me that I would have to begin earning money, I've been watching different farmers to see what they do to earn money. I have noticed that some of them, like you, raise cattle to sell, and others, like Mr. Brown, raise hogs to sell. Now I would like to do something of this sort myself."

"You certainly have studied everything very carefully," said Mr. Penney.

Jimmy continued, "I don't know how much a pig will cost. Possibly I'll have to save more before I can buy one, but I thought that I should get your permission first."

Mr. Penney smiled. He wondered how Jimmy would get money to care for the pig but decided not to inquire now. He simply would grant permission to buy the pig and let him work out this problem later. "All right, go ahead," he said in an encouraging tone of voice.

"Thank you, Father," said Jimmy. "Now I have one more question to ask. May I build a pen in the back yard for the pig?"

"Yes," replied Mr. Penney. "You'll find plenty of old lumber out there for building a pen. If need be, you may put your pig in my pen until you get your pen built."

The next day Jimmy went to Mr. Brown's farm where he had noticed some little pigs running about. "Mr. Brown," he said excitedly, "I have been working to earn money, and now I would like to purchase one of your little pigs."

94

"I don't understand," said Mr. Brown. "Why do you want to buy a pig?"

"I want to raise the pig to grow into a big hog," replied Jimmy. "Then I can sell it for more money than I'll have to pay for it. In that way I'll make my money earn more money."

"Well, for an eight-year-old boy you certainly have planned well," chuckled Mr. Brown. "I would like to favor you, but I never sell any little pigs. Always I keep them to grow into big hogs so I can sell them for more money."

"Please, Mr. Brown," pleaded Jimmy, "let me buy one. I have two dollars and fifty cents to pay you for one."

Mr. Brown couldn't resist Jimmy's eager voice and pleading blue-gray eyes. One of his pigs really was worth more than two dollars and fifty cents, but he was willing to sell Jimmy the pig at a sacrifice. He liked Jimmy and wanted to help him carry on his worthy project.

After Mr. Brown agreed to sell Jimmy a pig, he asked, "Where do you expect to keep the pig when you get home?"

"I'm going to build a pen back of our house, but to begin with my father said that I could keep it in his pen," replied Jimmy. "Raising a pig is my own project and has nothing to do with my father's work. He told me that I could buy a pig and build a pen for it."

"I have another question," said Mr. Brown, looking down at the grateful boy before him. "You have agreed to pay me two dollars and fifty cents for the pig, which is all the money you have. Without having any money left, how do you plan to buy feed for the pig?"

Again Jimmy surprised Mr. Brown by having a quick answer. "Father has a hog in a pen in our back yard which he is getting ready to butcher," he explained. "Mother saves left-over bits of food from the table, potato peelings and other scraps from the kitchen, and scrapings from pots and pans, which she puts into a slop bucket to feed to the hog. Now some of our neighbors have to pay to have their slop or garbage hauled away because they have no hogs in

their back yards. I plan to offer to haul away their slop and to clean their slop buckets every day just to get plenty of feed for my pig. Does this sound like a good plan to you?"

"Yes, indeed, Jimmy," replied Mr. Brown. "You have planned everything well, and I hope you enjoy raising your new pig."

Mr. Brown, like many friendly farmers, was glad to encourage a boy interested in caring for farm animals. In order to help Jimmy, he willingly sold him a pig for less than it really was worth and sought to offer him helpful advice.

Raising a Pig
for Profit

"WILL FATHER's big hog harm my little pig during the night? Will my little pig become so homesick in its strange pen that it will try to root its way out?" These and other similar questions kept Jimmy awake much of the first night that he owned his new pig.

The next morning he could hardly wait for the sun to peek through the spaces between the houses in Hamilton. He dressed hurriedly and slipped out quietly to check on his little pig in the back yard. "Here, piggy, piggy!" he called softly. "Here, piggy, piggy!"

The little pig came running to the side of the

pen. Jimmy was surprised that it came running so quickly. "Gee, you know me already," he said. "Now be good today and maybe tonight you can sleep in a pen of your own."

After Jimmy was certain the pig was all right, he hurried back into the house. By now his mother had started to get breakfast in the kitchen. "Why, Jimmy, what are you doing coming in the back door at this hour in the morning?" she asked in a surprised tone of voice. "Usually at this hour you are just going out to milk the cow. Possibly you got up early this morning and have already done the milking."

Jimmy grinned. "Yes, I know, Mother," he explained. "I've been out checking on my little pig. I wanted to see whether it is still alive and still there. I got up early because I don't want to let taking care of my pig interfere with doing my chores. Now I'm ready to do the milking and have come in to wash my hands."

Jimmy finished washing his hands and quickly left the house again. He hurriedly milked the cow and brought the pail of milk to the house. At breakfast the family teased him about how rapidly he was doing his work.

This was an important day for Jimmy. He wanted to begin building his new pen as early as possible in order to finish it before night. He rushed from the house and pulled out suitable posts and boards from a stack of old lumber in the back yard. He dug deep holes and set the posts securely in the ground. Then he nailed the boards to the posts close together to keep the pig from crawling out.

After he finished the pen, he made a small trough for feeding the pig, but realized that he would have to fasten it down to keep the pig from upsetting it. He looked at the trough in his father's pen and found that he had driven stakes in the ground to hold the trough in place.

Then he went to his trough and drove stakes in the ground to hold it in place in the same way. "I'm certainly fortunate to have a father who knows how to do things," he thought.

After he had completed both the pen and the trough, he started out to see whether he could find some feed for the pig. He knocked at the kitchen door of a nearby house, and a woman came to the door. "No, Jimmy," she called out, "I don't need you to run any errands for me this afternoon."

"Oh, I came for something different today," explained Jimmy. "I came to ask whether I can have the left-over scraps of food in your slop bucket. I'll pick them up regularly every afternoon and bring back the bucket washed out clean for you."

"Surely you may have my left-over scraps," said the woman curiously, "but please tell me why in the world you want them."

102

"Well, I have to earn money to buy my own clothes, and I'm trying to raise a pig to sell," explained Jimmy. "My mother saves all the left-over scraps in our slop bucket to feed a hog that my father is getting ready to butcher. Now I'm trying to get left-over scraps away from home to feed to my pig."

"You are a very smart boy to think of getting feed for your pig in this way," said the neighbor woman. "I'll be pleased to have you pick up my left-over scraps every afternoon and to bring the slop bucket back clean. This arrangement will be helpful to both of us."

Every afternoon from now on Jimmy carried the slop bucket from the neighbor woman's back porch and emptied it into the trough in his pig pen. Sometimes it was so brimming full that he had to walk very slowly to keep from spilling it. Always he was careful to stop and pick up any scraps that happened to fall out.

For an eight-year-old boy this task of picking up and scrubbing a dirty slop bucket was very unpleasant, but Jimmy kept on fulfilling his agreement. He felt grateful to the neighbor woman for helping him to get feed for his pig and wanted to keep on doing his part.

Jimmy's choice of feed for the pig was very practical. The pig served as a disposal for left-over scraps of food, and these left-overs made the pig grow. During the following weeks the pig became larger and larger.

In the meantime Jimmy had kept on doing odd jobs in the community to earn money. He didn't let caring for the pig interfere with doing whatever work he could find. At times he became discouraged because he couldn't increase his earnings more rapidly, but he found it comforting to be raising a pig. Someday, if all went well, he would be able to make money by selling his fast-growing pig for profit.

After Jimmy's pig grew into a big hog, he faced the problem of fattening it for market. He took the problem to his father. "I notice that you are feeding your hog corn in order to fatten it for butchering," he said. "Now I'll soon have to feed my hog corn to fatten it for market. How soon should I begin to feed it?"

"That's a good question, Jimmy," replied Mr. Penney. "I wondered whether you would realize that you'll have to fatten your hog. You should begin to feed it corn about the first week in October. Then you should have it fattened and ready to sell sometime in November, when it's about six months old."

"October is not far away," said Jimmy. "I'll soon have to buy some corn."

"Well, I think I can save you some money," offered Mr. Penney. "Instead of buying corn you may pick up scattered ears in my cornfield which we have overlooked in harvesting."

106

"Oh, boy, that's great, Father!" exclaimed Jimmy. "Do you mean that I may have the corn free, just for picking it up?"

"That's right," replied Mr. Penney. "If you start to collect the corn now, you should have enough saved to fatten the hog by the time you will need it."

The following Saturday, Jimmy got up early to do his morning chores. He planned to ride out to the farm with his father to begin looking for corn. He hoped to bring back a bushel or two to store away for his hog.

Mr. Penney usually planted only one field of corn because he needed his land for pasture. He raised the corn merely to feed to his cattle, not to sell. Often he had to buy additional corn to get his cattle ready for market.

Jimmy was thankful to be able to pick up the scattered ears of corn. He was surprised to find how many ears had been left from harvesting.

He made several trips to the farm and soon had more corn than he would need.

Before long he began to feel sad about having to sell the hog, which now had become almost a pet. As the time drew near for taking the hog to market, he said, "I just don't think I can part with it. I'll miss feeding it and having it come grunting to meet me."

He overcame his grief about parting with the hog by thinking of the matter seriously. He had not raised the hog as a pet but as an investment to earn money. He realized that all farmers come to love their animals and enjoy taking care of them. At the same time they raise their animals for income and must be willing to sell them whenever they are ready for market. They cannot let their sentiments keep them from parting with animals that are ready to sell.

A few days later Jimmy and his father took his hog to market. On the way he tried to be brave just as if he were a real farmer taking his stock to market. His face brightened as the stock buyer started to count out a handful of one dollar bills to pay for the hog.

When Jimmy reached home he proudly showed his money to his mother. At once she said, "What do you intend to do with so much money?"

Then Jimmy explained. He already had definite plans for using it. First he would purchase some new clothes which he needed for school during the winter. Then he would save the rest of the money to buy two little pigs the following spring. His investment had paid off and he was eager to make a bigger investment.

He had sold his pig for a profit. Now he would grow more pigs to sell.

The Buyer Beware

One late fall day Mr. Penney said, "I have been too busy lately to go to purchase a wagonload of firewood. Now that you are past ten years old, you should be able to choose a good load for me. Tomorrow you may go to purchase a load of wood."

The people of Hamilton depended on the farmers nearby for firewood to burn in their fireplaces and stoves. These farmers cut wood from the wooded parts of their farms and brought wagonloads to a vacant lot in Hamilton to sell. Several times a year, especially in winter, Mr. Penney went to the lot to purchase firewood.

Early the next morning Jimmy hastened to the vacant lot to begin examining wagonloads of firewood. He went from wagon to wagon. He tried to decide which loads were best. Suddenly he heard his friend Carl Pickell calling from the street, "What are you doing here?"

"I'm trying to pick out a good wagonload of firewood to buy," said Jimmy. "Come on and help me, if you have time."

Carl came to join Jimmy. "Why didn't your father rather than you come to pick out the firewood?" he asked. "My father always comes to pick out our firewood."

"Well, my father has been very busy lately and asked me to come in his place," replied Jimmy. "This is the first time I have ever tried to pick out a load of firewood, so I'm working very cautiously. First I'm trying to decide which loads of wood are the best. Then later I'll inquire about the prices."

"Well, we both have handled enough firewood around our homes to know what to look for," commented Carl.

"Yes, we should look for chunks that are straight and free from knots," explained Jimmy. "Straight chunks are much easier to split than chunks that contain knots. Besides, they stack up better and are easier to handle."

The boys checked all the wagonloads of firewood and finally selected a few loads that seemed to be better than the others. Then Carl had to leave to finish running some errands for his mother. "Thank you for stopping to help me," said Jimmy. "Now I'll go back to see which load I can buy at the best price."

He went back to talk over prices with the farmers who had the best loads of firewood. He asked each farmer for a price to include delivering the wood to his home. Soon he and a farmer agreed on a reasonable price.

112

"Now I'll tell you where to deliver the load of firewood," he said. "We live in a white frame house located at 201 East Bird Street. It's only a block away from the railroad track and only a block from Davis Street, where most of the stores are. Oh, well, since I'm ready to go home anyhow, I'll just climb on your wagon and go along to show you the way."

When they arrived at the Penney home, Jimmy pointed the way around the house to the woodshed. He hurried back to help the farmer unload the chunks of wood from the wagon and stack them up in the woodshed. Then he paid the farmer and went proudly into the house to report how well he had done.

Later that afternoon he went to the woodshed to split some of the chunks of wood. Suddenly he heard a voice in the street calling, "Firewood! Buy your firewood cheap."

He ran to the front of the house to see what

was going on. There he found a farmer with a wagonload of firewood just as good as that which he had purchased. When the farmer saw him coming, he stopped his horses and called, "Sonny, do your folks need a load of wood?"

"No, sir, they don't," replied Jimmy.

"Are you sure?" urged the farmer. "They can have this load real cheap."

Jimmy looked at the farmer. "What do you mean by cheap?" he asked

"Well, I'll sell it delivered to your woodshed for half of what I asked for it this morning," replied the farmer.

Jimmy was surprised by this offer. "That seems strange," he said. "Why are you willing to sell it so much cheaper now?"

"There just weren't enough people at the lot today to buy all the firewood," explained the farmer. "Now I would rather sell my load at half price than take it back home."

114

Jimmy was dazed. Here was a chance to buy a load of wood for half as much as he had already paid. Now it was too late, and he wondered whether he had bought his load too soon. Sadly he watched the farmer drive on down the street, calling, "Wood for sale!"

During supper Jimmy solemnly told his father about the opportunity to buy a load of firewood at half the price he had paid for a load earlier in the day. Mr. Penney felt sorry for him and tried to explain. "This can happen in buying any kind of merchandise—shoes, suits, or wood," he said. "Merchants often cut prices when they have merchandise left over."

"Yes, I know," replied Jimmy, "but I don't like to be offered a cut price so soon after I have paid the regular price. I feel guilty about having paid twice as much for the load of firewood this morning as I would have had to pay for a load later in the afternoon."

"Don't feel guilty, son," said Mr. Penney sympathetically. "You did right in choosing the load of firewood at the best price you could when there were many loads to choose from. Ordinarily when someone reduces the price of wood late in the day, it is of poor quality."

Jimmy was relieved to know that his father didn't feel he had committed a blunder. Later when he went up to his room, he carried a copy of *Youth's Companion* which had come in the morning mail. He wanted to read some of the stories before he went to bed.

The months rolled by, and Jimmy continued to buy and sell pigs. Out of his profits he spent only what money he needed for buying new clothes. The rest of his profits he invested in more and more pigs.

During the two years after he had purchased his first pig, he increased his number of pigs to eleven, all of which he kept in the pen in the

116

back yard. Now he had to carry slop buckets from a dozen homes in order to get enough feed for the pigs. Mr. and Mrs. Penney were very proud of him because he kept everything well organized in taking care of the pigs. They only hoped that little Herbie, who had been born a few months before, would grow up to be equally self-reliant.

When the hot summer days came, Jimmy found carrying the dirty slop buckets a very sickening job, but he never neglected his work. He felt that this unpleasant work was necessary in order to help the pigs grow into big hogs. In the fall he would be rewarded by being able to sell his big hogs at a profit.

One August evening as Jimmy finished washing the buckets, Mr. Penney suddenly came around the corner of the house. "Jimmy, I want to talk with you for a few minutes before you return the slop buckets," he abruptly announced.

"All right, Father," replied Jimmy, alarmed by the serious tone of his father's voice. He could tell that Mr. Penney was about to give him some unexpected orders.

Mr. Penney motioned for him to sit down beside him on the steps of the back porch. Then he spoke bluntly. "Tonight when you return the slop buckets, tell the owners that you won't pick them up any more. Tomorrow you'll have to sell all your pigs."

Jimmy was stunned. He usually didn't interrupt his father, but this time he exclaimed, "Oh, no, Father! Why, my pigs are only half grown and this is the wrong time of the year to sell pigs at a profit."

"I know, but you have no other choice," replied Mr. Penney. "Some of the neighbors have complained about your keeping so many pigs in our back yard. They didn't object when you kept only one or two pigs, but they think that

119

eleven pigs are entirely too many. They object to the stench that comes from the pen and the terrible odor of the slop that you use for feed."

Jimmy hung his head, but he tried not to show how badly he was hurt. Mr. Penney continued, "We live in a town where the people take great pride in keeping their homes neat and clean. Most of them don't keep even a single pig in their back yards. For this reason you can understand how they feel about your having eleven pigs. We must always do unto others as we would have them do unto us."

The next morning Jimmy went into the country to try to sell his half-grown pigs. Soon he found a farmer who was willing to give him sixty dollars for the pigs. As he walked back to town, he had a great mixture of feelings. He was humiliated about the neighbors' complaints and disappointed because he had to sell his pigs before they were ready for market.

When Jimmy received the sixty dollars for his pigs, he realized that he would have to make this money last for a long time. It was nearly time for him to start to school again and he would have little opportunity to earn money during the school year.

One of his greatest problems was to decide where he could keep the money safely. He reached a conclusion quickly, however, as he walked past the two banks in Hamilton. He would deposit thirty dollars in one bank and thirty dollars in the other bank. He had heard grown-ups talk about banks failing sometimes and causing people to lose all their savings. He would take only half this chance by depositing his sixty dollars in two different banks.

This simple act on Jimmy's part showed that he fast was developing a good business sense. His father was pleased with his growing ability both to make money and to save it.

An Honest Horse Trader

"FATHER, may I have a short talk with you after we finish eating supper?" asked Jimmy in a serious tone of voice. "I have something important to discuss with you."

"Why, yes, come out to the back steps," replied Mr. Penney. "You sound as if you have a serious problem, but possibly I can help you."

Jimmy laughed. "No, my problem isn't exactly serious, but it's important," he explained. "Perhaps I could call it a 'dire need.'"

"Well, every problem calls for a solution," said Mr. Penney, seating himself on the steps. "What do you mean by a dire need?"

"I mean that I need a horse to ride out in the country so that I can take jobs farther from home," explained Jimmy. "First, I want to know whether you'll let me get a horse and keep it here to ride out to work day after day. Second, I wonder whether you'll be willing to buy a good horse for me."

Mr. Penney leaned against the post of the porch and started to laugh. "I'm glad to know, son, that your only dire need is the need for a horse," he said. "Why, of course you may buy a horse and keep it here, but don't expect me to pay for it."

"Oh, I didn't mean for you to pay for it," explained Jimmy. "I merely meant that I wanted you to pick it out for me, not pay for it. I'll pay for it myself."

"No, Jimmy, now that you are twelve years old I think you are old enough to pick out your own horse. As I have told you many times in the past, it's good for you to figure things out for yourself. You need to have to make decisions without relying on someone else. Now let me tell you some things that you may find helpful in buying a horse."

For a long time Mr. Penney and Jimmy sat on the back steps together. Mr. Penney carefully explained to Jimmy many important things to consider in choosing a good horse. Finally he warned him not to believe everything an owner might say about a horse.

Jimmy was amazed as his father told him about some of the tricks a horse trader might use in order to deceive him about a horse. He hoped that he could remember all these tricks so that he wouldn't be cheated. He wanted to be sure to purchase a good horse.

"Thank you, Father, for all the information," he said gratefully. "If I need to ask any further questions, I'll come to you again. Purchas-

124

ing a horse will be a big investment for me, and I can't afford to make a mistake."

"Well, I wish you luck, but be especially wary," said Mr. Penney. "There seems to be little honor among horse traders. You should do all right, however, because so far you have done a good job of buying and selling."

For several days Jimmy canvassed the nearby country to find horses for sale. He looked at all the horses very carefully. Finally he found a pretty two-year-old mare which caught his eye. She was running loose in a field.

The owner explained that the mare had been broken for riding. She had no bridle on her head or saddle on her back, but Jimmy climbed on her back to take a little ride. He clung on by holding tightly to her mane and guided her by patting her neck. She seemed to be pleased to have him riding her. Finally he called, "Whoa," and she stopped to let him off.

"Sir, I think I'll take this little mare," said Jimmy. "May I borrow a piece of rope to use as a halter for leading her home? I'll return the rope tomorrow."

"Oh, I'll gladly give you a piece of rope for leading her home," replied the farmer, "and you won't have to return it." He was amused that Jimmy offered to bring it back.

The man made a halter out of the rope, and Jimmy proudly led the little mare home. He arrived just as his mother was preparing to put supper on the table. Mr. Penney, Elie, Mittie, and Pearl all rushed out to see the new horse. "What do you think of her, Father?" asked Jimmy eagerly.

Mr. Penney looked over the mare very carefully. He wondered whether Jimmy had remembered things he had told him several nights before. "Well, as nearly as I can tell," he finally replied, "you have done a very good job of

126

choosing your first horse. I am proud of you for picking her out all by yourself."

Mrs. Penney called to Mr. Penney and the others from the door, "Come on in to supper. Your evening meal is getting cold on the table. Put the new horse in the barn. Then you can go back to look at her after you finish eating."

Jimmy promptly led the little mare around the house to the barn and tied her in a stall. Then quickly he shut the door and ran back to the house for supper.

Soon all members of the family sat down at the table with heads bowed for Mr. Penney's evening devotions. Just as he started to pray, everybody at the table heard loud thumping sounds coming from the barn. He continued to pray even though he was interrupted by sounds of *thump, thump, thump* coming with great regularity from the barn. Jimmy was worried but knew that he had to remain quiet.

Finally, when Mr. Penney said "Amen," Jimmy said quietly, "I'm worried about those thumping sounds coming from the barn. May I go out there to see what is happening?"

"Of course," replied Mr. Penney. "Your new mare probably is frightened by her new surroundings and is kicking the end of the stall. Perhaps you can quiet her by talking to her softly and by patting her head gently."

Jimmy dashed out the back door and down the short path to the barn. He opened the barn door and found the little mare kicking the end of her stall, just as his father had suspected. He hurried to the front of the stall and started to talk to her. He reached forward and patted her head. Nothing he did seemed to quiet her. She just kept on kicking and kicking.

Finally Jimmy gave up trying and returned to the house. His mother called him to join the other members of the family at the table.

128

"Come and eat, Jimmy," she said softly. "Then you can look after your mare later."

Jimmy sat down at the table, but he was more eager to talk than to eat. "Father," he said, "I just can't get that mare to stop kicking. I tried talking to her and patting her head, as you suggested, but she wouldn't stop. She'll wear herself out acting this way. What shall I do about her?"

"Just be patient," advised Mr. Penney. "Perhaps she'll settle down after she becomes used to the stall. I have heard of horses acting that way when they are first put into a barn, if they have been kept out in a field. Most horses today, however, are used to being kept in barns. Did you ask the owner where he has kept the mare?"

"No, I didn't think of it," replied Jimmy.

"Nor did I think to tell you," said Mr. Penney. "Something like this happens so seldom

129

that it completely slipped my mind. You found the mare in a field, and she may always have lived there. The owner even may have known that she didn't like to be in a barn. If you didn't ask, he didn't have to tell you."

All evening the mare kept kicking. Before bedtime Jimmy and his father went to the barn to attempt to quiet her. Finally Mr. Penney said, "We might as well give up and return to the house. I had hoped she would quiet down because her constant kicking will keep the whole neighborhood awake tonight."

Back in the house Jimmy went to bed very downhearted about his new mare. He lay in bed and tried to go to sleep, but he could hear her kicking *thump, thump, thump*. At last he dozed off, but the first thing the next morning he heard her still kicking *thump, thump, thump*. At breakfast he asked, "Father, do you think she kicked that way all night?"

130

"No, she probably stopped for a while, but evidently started again early today," replied Mr. Penney. "Possibly before the end of the day she will become too tired to keep on kicking. I suggest that you take her out for a long ride this morning. Put my bridle on her and ride out toward the farm."

The little mare seemed to be happy when Jimmy led her out of the stall. She didn't shake her head or fight when he put the bridle on her. She even stood still when he threw a sack over her back to use as a saddle.

Jimmy enjoyed riding the little mare. She responded promptly when he spoke to her or pulled on the reins. She trotted along the road unafraid of dogs or children or other distractions that sometimes frighten horses.

As Jimmy rode the little mare, he kept talking to her. "Everything will be all right with you now," he said. "You probably have just

been afraid of your stall. Today I'll ride you around the countryside, so you'll get plenty of exercise. Then when I take you back and put you into your stall, you'll be too tired to kick. You'll just be happy to rest."

132

Jimmy's efforts were in vain. When he put the little mare back, she immediately began kicking again. Once more he talked soothingly to her, but she paid no attention to him.

For several days Jimmy tried the same routine, but without success. Finally one evening after supper he and his father had another conversation. "You seem to have tried every possible way to get the little mare to settle down in her stall," said Mr. Penney, "but she simply won't do it. You can't turn her loose here in our yard, so you'll just have to sell her."

"I'm afraid so," replied Jimmy seriously, "but how can I get anyone to buy her when she acts like that? I'll probably have to take a big loss to get rid of her."

"Yes, you may not get more than half what you paid for her," replied Mr. Penney, "because you'll have to tell the truth about her. You can't let anybody think she's broken to stay in

133

a barn when she isn't. You just haven't been brought up that way."

Jimmy found taking a loss on the little mare a bitter business experience. Buying and selling a horse, like buying and selling pigs, had turned out to be a bad business venture. Somehow it seemed to him that the older he became the less successful he was in buying and selling. Now that he was twelve years old, he thought that he should do better.

Even so, he did not become discouraged. He simply set up goals to do better in the future. He would use his experience to advantage by trying to avoid making the same mistakes again.

Watermelons for Sale

"Jimmy, you seem to be somewhat interested in farming," said Mr. Penney one late winter day. "How would you like to have the use of a few acres of land this spring and summer? You can grow any kind of crop that you think will sell. About your only expense will be the money that you'll have to spend for seed."

Mr. Penney watched closely to see how his twelve-year-old son would react to this offer. "If you think you are interested," he continued, "we can go out to the farm some Saturday morning soon to mark off your land."

Jimmy hesitated. "Thank you, Father," he

said. "Right now I think I would like to accept your offer, but I would like to think about it further before I decide."

"Well, it's still late winter, so you have a few weeks to decide," said Mr. Penney.

For several days Jimmy pondered the idea of growing a crop. He was almost certain that he wanted to try it, but was uncertain what crop would be the most profitable to grow. Finally he settled on watermelons.

One night at the supper table he announced, "Father, I have decided to accept your offer, and I want to try growing watermelons. What do you think of my choice?"

At first Mr. Penney was dumbfounded by Jimmy's selection of a crop. He leaned back his head and stared blankly at the ceiling for a moment before answering. "Well, I'm somewhat surprised with your selection," he said, "but there are no strings attached to my offer."

"Will you let me have a big piece of water-melon to eat?" asked six-year-old Pearl.

"Yes, and you may have a big piece, too," he said, patting his two-year-old brother Herbie on the head.

A few weeks later, Jimmy went out to the farm with Mr. Penney and picked out four acres for growing watermelons. He chose a spot next to the road, because he hoped to sell some of his watermelons to people passing by. He thought particularly of coal miners who walked past the field to and from their work at a nearby coal mine. For some years Mr. Penney had leased some of his land to a coal mining company that operated the mine.

After there was no further danger of frost, Jimmy plowed his plot of ground and carefully planted the watermelon seeds. He diligently tended the plants as they extended themselves into vines, and little watermelons began to form

137

on the vines. From then on the biggest problem was to wait patiently until the watermelons would grow and ripen.

As the watermelons began to ripen, he went out to the farm nearly every day. He spotted a few watermelons that seemed to be ripening ahead of the others. "I'll take the very first ripe watermelon home for Pearl and Herbie to eat," he said to himself.

The next morning Jimmy went happily along the rows to check on the few watermelons that seemed to be ripening ahead of the others. When he came to the spot where he expected to find the first watermelon, he was surprised to find no watermelon there. "I must have miscounted the rows," he said to himself.

He stood up and carefully checked the rows between himself and the fence. "One, two, three, four, five," he counted. "Yes, this is the spot, but the watermelon is gone." He checked the rows where he had found the other water-melons ripening and discovered that those wa-termelons were gone, too. "Someone must have stolen them," he said.

This was a hard blow to Jimmy, because it had never occurred to him that somebody might steal his watermelons. Within a few days many, many more of his watermelons would ripen. What could he do to protect them?

He decided to walk into town rather than to wait to ride with his father. He wanted an opportunity to think seriously about what he should do. By the time he reached home he had come to a decision. He would spend the nights camping out at the farm and would take the family dog and his gun along for protection.

When Mr. Penney reached home, Jimmy im-mediately explained his plan. "I can't take chances on people stealing my watermelons," he said, "so I have decided to spend the nights camping out at the farm. I would like to take our dog and my gun with me to help scare people away. May I rent your cart to haul my things out to the farm?"

Mr. Penney was pleased with the thoughtful way in which Jimmy had solved his problem. "You won't need to rent my cart for hauling your things to the farm," he said. "After supper I'll take them out for you. Possibly Herbie and Pearl will want to go along for a ride."

That evening Mr. Penney took Jimmy with his tent, bedding, and other things out to the farm. Pearl and Herbie, too, crowded into the cart and the family dog followed. Soon Mr. Penney and the children headed back, leaving Jimmy alone with the dog.

At once Jimmy put up his tent at one edge of the watermelon patch and made his bed in the tent. He left one end of the tent open so he could look out over the patch. He laid his

140

gun within easy reach and gave the dog in-
structions to lie down beside him.

Jimmy was very sleepy as he settled down
in his tent. He tried to stay awake by talking
to the dog, but even the dog seemed to be
sleepy. Before long a wagon rolled along the
road in front of the watermelon patch. The
dog immediately jumped up and ran barking
toward the wagon. He stopped at the fence
along the patch but kept on barking noisily.

After the wagon disappeared, the dog came
running back to the tent. He rushed up to
Jimmy to obtain a pat of approval. Jimmy
reached over, stroked the dog's head, and said,
"You're going to be a good watchdog, just as I
knew you would be. Now that you are watching things well, I can take a little snooze."

Jimmy relaxed his tense watching and soon
went fast asleep. From then on everything re-
mained quiet until it was time for the miners

to start going home from their late shift at the coal mine. The dog was greatly disturbed when he heard all the men going by and ran barking loudly to the fence.

Jimmy awoke startled, not realizing what was going on. Still half asleep, he jumped to the conclusion that someone was stealing his melons. He yelled as loudly as he could, "Stop! Stop, whoever you are! I have a gun. Leave my watermelons alone, or I'll shoot!"

As soon as he could get to his feet, he picked up his gun, dashed outside, and fired a shot into the air. The miners were taken by complete surprise and were afraid that he might shoot in their direction. "Hold your fire!" shouted one from the road.

"Don't shoot again!" shouted another.

"We're only miners on our way home," explained a third. "We're not climbing the fence to get any of your melons!"

142

Night after night Jimmy stayed at the farm to watch his watermelons, but nobody tried to steal them. As they began to ripen, few people stopped at the patch to buy them. Finally he borrowed his father's horse and wagon and drove from house to house about the town, crying, "Watermelons for sale!"

By now it was time for the county fair which would be held in Hamilton. The fair would last for a week and people for miles around would come to the fair.

Jimmy decided to try selling his watermelons at the fair, where he could reach many possible buyers at one time. Most people brought picnic lunches to eat at the fair, and he was sure that some of them would want to buy watermelons to add to their lunches.

Early on the first day of the fair, he filled the wagon with his largest and ripest watermelons and headed for the fairground. As he rode along he wondered where he should park the wagon so that his melons would attract the most attention. As he approached the entrance gate, he noticed many wagons and buggies lined up, waiting their turns to get in. At once he decided that a place here, off to one side outside the entrance gate, would be a good place to park. Then all the people would pass him as they waited in line to get inside.

Jimmy readily found a place for his wagon right where he wanted to be. Then he stood beside the wagon and called out loudly, "Watermelons for sale! Ladies and gentlemen, have watermelon with your picnic lunch today! Buy a big juicy watermelon here for one thin dime, only one-tenth of a dollar! That's all it takes to get a big juicy watermelon!"

Normally Jimmy was rather shy, but he felt that he should try to drown out the singsong chants of barkers calling to customers inside the fairgrounds. Many people came to his wagon to purchase watermelons before they entered the grounds. He treated them courteously, helped them to choose good watermelons to eat, and thanked them for coming. At the same time, he kept up his chant, "Ten cents for large watermelons, five cents for small ones!"

All was going well, and Jimmy was very busy selling when suddenly he heard his father calling loudly, "'James Cash Penney! Stop selling and get ready to go home."

Jimmy was shocked by these words. He looked around and saw Mr. Penney close beside the horse preparing to unhitch the horse from the fence. He wondered why his father was ordering him to go home, but he knew better than to ask. From many previous experiences when his father had issued orders, he had learned to obey without asking questions.

Jimmy climbed on the wagon and slowly started home with the team and wagon. He didn't have far to go, but it seemed like a long way because he was eager to find out what was wrong. When he stopped at the house, Mr. Penney came walking to the wagon and said, "Young man, I certainly was embarrassed to find you selling watermelons at the fair today."

"Why, Father?" asked Jimmy, bewildered. "I was doing a good honest business. I wasn't cheating anybody or doing anything to be ashamed of. I was selling my watermelons at the same prices as I have been selling them around town."

"Well, persons aren't allowed to sell things at the fair unless they pay for the rights to sell," explained Mr. Penney. "Since the rights are expensive, I felt sure that you hadn't paid for the privilege of selling there."

"No, I hadn't," replied Jimmy, "but I didn't know that a person had to buy rights in order to sell. Anyhow, I wasn't selling to people on the fairgrounds. I was selling to them outside before they went through the entrance."

"Yes, I know," said Mr. Penney, "but by selling outside you were cheating the people who paid to sell inside."

"I'm sorry, Father, but I just didn't know

any better," explained Jimmy solemnly. "I certainly wouldn't want to cheat anyone and hope you will forgive me for embarrassing you."

"Well, I hated to stop you so abruptly," said Mr. Penney in a kindly tone of voice, "but I just couldn't let you go on selling outside when others had paid to sell inside."

Jimmy sat on his wagon for a long time thinking. He was greatly disappointed, but realized that all was not lost. He still could sell his watermelons a few at a time by driving along the streets. His father was right about not allowing him to sell outside the fairgrounds, but he certainly had lost an opportunity to reach many buyers all in one spot.

Soon he started off again down the streets of Hamilton, calling, "Buy big juicy watermelons here for only one thin dime, only one-tenth of a dollar!" He still would find customers going to the fair, but not all in one place.

A Merchant's Helper

ONE SUMMER DAY in 1893, a few months after Jimmy had graduated from high school, he and Elie were working on Mr. Penney's farm. "Elie, may I ride home with you this afternoon?" Jimmy asked. "I want to talk with you."

"Certainly," replied Elie. "I'll be glad to have you ride with me."

As they rode home, Jimmy talked seriously with Elie about his future. "I have graduated from Hamilton High School and am going on eighteen years of age," he said, "yet I don't know what I want to do in life. You're twenty-eight years old, and you have bought a farm and plan to be married soon. Now I hoped that you could give me some advice."

"I thought you planned to go to college," said Elie. "Once I heard you say that you'd like to become a lawyer or a preacher."

"Yes, but now I'm not certain," explained Jimmy. "For one thing, I didn't earn very good grades in high school. For another, I haven't saved enough money to go to college. If I keep on working at odd jobs around here, it will take me some time to save enough money to pay for more schooling."

"Well, I'm afraid that I can't advise you," said Elie, "but I can help you to get work. Our parents have a farm, Mittie and her husband have a farm, and I have a farm. Between the three farms in the family, you may be sure of plenty of work to do."

For over a year and a half after Jimmy graduated from high school, he continued to work and save money, but he failed to stay on any particular job. Finally, during the second winter after his graduation, his father became ill. As Mr. Penney lay in bed, he thought seriously about the welfare of his children. From his sick bed he concluded that Jimmy should get a job buying and selling. He felt that Jimmy was best suited to this kind of work.

Finally Mr. Penney thought of a plan to get Jimmy a job as a clerk in a store where he could learn to become a merchant. Acting on this idea, he climbed out of his sick bed and went to see Mr. J. M. Hale, owner of J. M. Hale and Brother, a dry goods store in Hamilton.

"Mr. Hale," said Mr. Penney, "I would like to have you take my boy Jimmy in your store and teach him the fundamentals of business. He is a hard worker and will do a good job for you working for you. I'll appreciate anything that you can do for him."

"Well, I already have six clerks and really don't need another one," said Mr. Hale. "On the other hand, I would like to do both you and Jimmy a favor. If he wants to work here to learn retailing, I'll gladly pay him twenty-five dollars for the rest of the year. That isn't much, but I'll be glad to teach him all I can. In case he wants the job, tell him he can start on February fourth."

Mr. Penney returned home and told Jimmy about the opportunity for him to work for Mr. Hale to learn the retailing business. "Do you think you will want to accept?" he asked.

Jimmy didn't hesitate. "Sure, I'll accept," he replied enthusiastically. "It's a fine opportunity, and I appreciate your getting out and making the arrangements for me."

When Jimmy reported for work the first morning, he expected the other clerks to help him learn what to do, especially to sell goods over the counters. On the contrary, they resented his being there and failed to cooperate with him. They tried to prevent his selling goods over the counters, and some of them even poked fun at him. Often when he was waiting on a customer, an older salesman would come up with the flimsy explanation that Mr. Hale had sent him to take over the selling.

Jimmy was discouraged, but he continued to work hard on the job. He decided that he could afford to put up with the abuse just to learn the business. Since he had little opportunity to sell, he devoted more and more time to looking after the stock. He put articles away after clerks and customers had left them lying on the counters. He unpacked articles, put them on the shelves, and labeled them carefully. He learned to know all about merchandise.

At home he said nothing about his problems at the store. Both he and his mother were deeply worried about his father. Mr. Penney grew steadily worse and died at the age of fifty-three, a few weeks later.

Now Mrs. Penney and Jimmy had the burden of caring for the three younger children who were still at home. The youngest was Letha Mae, who was about four and a half years old. The two older were Herbert, who was nine, and Pearl, who was nearly thirteen.

Jimmy, now nineteen years old, felt a strong sense of responsibility for the family. He would have to make good working for Mr. Hale, because he would have to help support his mother and the three children.

Mrs. Penney bravely faced the burden that fell upon her after the early death of her husband. "You have mortgages on both your house and your farm," said a friend. "Why don't you sell the farm? Perhaps you could get enough money from it to pay off both mortgages."

Mrs. Penney had other ideas. "Jim and I were married over thirty years," she explained. "We had twelve children. The good Lord has seen fit to allow six of them to live to be with me now. Jim had great hopes for his farm, and now all of us will work together to make his land take care of us. We've all worked together before, and we'll work together again."

"I'll gladly stop working at Mr. Hale's store and try to take father's place on the farm," offered Jimmy.

"No, your father wanted you to learn merchandising," said Mrs. Penney. "He was already ill when he asked Mr. Hale to let you work there. He seemed to sense that he wasn't going to live and wanted to see you in work for which you are best suited. Elie and Mittie's husband can take care of the farm in addition to their farms. The important thing for you is to continue your training in the store."

From this time on nineteen-year-old Jimmy worked even harder at the store. He tried to learn all he could about the dry goods business. Already he was a very efficient stock boy. Frequently after the older clerks finished waiting on customers, they left the counters piled high with bolts of cloth which they had taken down to enable customers to pick out special colors or patterns. After they finished showing shoes to customers, they carelessly mixed up styles and sizes in the different shoe boxes.

Jimmy did not complain about the jumbled-up stock which he found. He put the bolts of cloth neatly back on the shelves and straightened out the shoes in the shoe boxes. All the while he learned more and more about the merchandise in the store. He learned where the items were, what the different qualities were, and what the different prices were.

He regretted not having a chance to sell.

Finally he made up his mind that he was going to be just as good a salesman as the other clerks in the store. After he made this decision, he started in with great determination.

When one of the older clerks tried to take a customer away from him, he politely but firmly said, "Mr. Hale wants me to take care of this customer, and I know just what the customer wants. Why don't you go ask Mr. Hale whether he wants you to do something else?"

At last Jimmy's efforts began to pay off. He made satisfied customers for the store. People liked him because he treated them courteously and because he knew the merchandise in the store. Mr. Hale carefully watched his work and was highly pleased with his efforts.

In accordance with Mr. Penney's arrangements with Mr. Hale, Jimmy received very little money for his work in the store. From February 4, 1895, to the end of the year, he earned only twenty-five dollars. When the first of January, 1896, rolled around, he expected Mr. Hale to say that he no longer would be needed at the store. Instead, Mr. Hale said, "You've done a very good job, Jimmy. Next year I'll pay you two hundred dollars for the full twelve months."

What a jump from twenty-five dollars to two hundred dollars! With this incentive, Jimmy began to work harder and harder. One year later, at the beginning of 1897, Mr. Hale raised his salary again. For his work the next year he would receive three hundred dollars.

During the winter of 1897, Jimmy developed an annoying cough that held on into the spring. Week after week he hoped his cough would get better, but instead it became steadily worse. Finally he developed a tired feeling along with the cough and decided to consult a doctor. "Jimmy," said the doctor after a thorough examination, "you'll have to stop working indoors. You need to spend more time outdoors, and it would be wise for you to move to some part of the country with a drier climate."

Jimmy was shocked by the doctor's diagnosis. "Do you mean that I have consumption?" he asked. Consumption was a name commonly used for the dreaded disease of tuberculosis, for which there was no known cure at that time.

"No, you don't actually have consumption, but with your body run down as it is, you might develop it," replied the doctor. "In your condition you need to exercise every possible precaution. I suggest that you stop working in the dry goods store immediately and that you move to some area with a drier climate, such as Denver, Colorado."

Jimmy left the doctor's office completely bewildered. He worried most about his mother, who needed his income to help support herself and the three children. How would she and Pearl, Herbie, and Letha manage without his being at home with them?

At first Jimmy was tempted not to tell his mother about the doctor's diagnosis and recommendation. Then he realized that she would be waiting for a report of what he had found out. He had no choice but to tell her.

Mrs. Penney reacted to the doctor's diagnosis and recommendation just as Jimmy had thought she would. "Often the Lord seems to bring obstacles into our way which we fail to understand," she said. "These obstacles merely are challenges which the Lord expects us to meet head-on. All of us must share in meeting this challenge which has come to you."

Later in the day, Jimmy went to tell Mr. Hale that he would have to give up his job. "Well, you certainly have been a valuable worker here," said Mr. Hale sympathetically.

"I'm sorry to have you leave, but of course you must follow the doctor's orders. Before you leave, I'll give you a strong letter of recommendation."

Back at home that night, Jimmy worked out definite plans with his mother to leave for Denver. "I have transferred three hundred dollars from my bank account to your bank account," he said seriously. "Don't worry about me because I have taken out enough money to buy my train ticket and to pay for my room and board for a while until I can find work."

Within a few days Jimmy boarded a train for Denver, Colorado. He was leaving both family and friends to go to live among strangers in a different part of the world. "What does the future hold for me?" he wondered.

The Golden Rule Stores

ALMOST IMMEDIATELY after young J. C. Penney arrived in Denver, Colorado, he started to look for work. Within a few hours he found a job as clerk in a dry goods store which paid him a salary of six dollars a week. He found a place to room and board nearby for four dollars and fifty cents a week. The difference between his salary and the cost of his room and board left him only one dollar and fifty cents per week for spending or saving.

During his first days at this dry goods store, he received the same sort of treatment from the older clerks as he had received from the older clerks at the J. M. Hale and Brother Store in Hamilton. They made fun of him and tried to take his customers away from him. By now, however, he knew how to defend himself, and they soon learned to leave him alone.

Later he worked at another store in Denver, but became eager to own his own business. Soon he heard of a butcher shop for sale at Longmont, Colorado, about forty miles north of Denver. He bought the butcher shop with three hundred dollars which he had left with his mother in Hamilton.

"I really don't know much about the butcher business," he said to himself, "but I know quite a bit about cattle. From watching my father run his cattle business, I should know how to buy cattle for butchering. Besides, being out in the open country part of the time will be good for my health."

A few days later young J. C. Penney stood

164

outside his new butcher shop, admiring a big bold sign on the front window. Near the top of the window was a large bull's head. Directly beneath the head was the name "J. C. Penney," and below the name were the words "Meat Market."

Young J. C. Penney felt very proud and grown-up as he looked at the sign. Few people in the West called him Jimmy. Now he was J. C. Penney, an adult, ready to face the world.

At first business was good in the butcher shop, and the best customer was a nearby hotel. Before long young Penney was notified that if he wanted to keep the hotel's business, he would have to give the chef a bottle of whiskey each week. Mr. Penney refused to enter into this sort of an arrangement and lost the hotel as a customer. A short time later, the butcher shop failed for lack of business.

Once again young Mr. Penney had to look

for a job. Already he had observed a dry goods store in Longmont, the Golden Rule Mercantile Company, where he felt he would like to work. Besides, he felt that he knew the dry goods business better than any other business. The manager of the store, T. M. Callahan, liked young Mr. Penney and said, "One of our clerks is sick and we'll need to hire a substitute for the Christmas season. Are you willing to take a temporary job?"

"I certainly will," replied Mr. Penney, "and I'll work just as hard as I would if you were hiring me for a permanent job."

Mr. Callahan had a partner in the Golden Rule Mercantile Company, named Guy Johnson, who managed a Golden Rule Store in Evanston, Wyoming. Together they owned a small chain of Golden Rule Stores in the Rocky Mountain area and planned to start several more. They would train promising young men

166

to become managers and later would help them to start other stores on a partnership basis.

Mr. Callahan watched young Mr. Penney at work in his store and came to regard him very highly. When the regular employee returned, Mr. Callahan suggested to Mr. Penney that he apply for a position with Mr. Johnson in Evanston. He explained that by going there Mr. Penney could take training to become a manager and might have an opportunity to start a store later.

In the spring of 1899 Mr. Penney went to Evanston to discuss this opportunity with Mr. Johnson. He impressed Mr. Johnson and was employed at a salary of fifty dollars a month. Now he was happy and hopeful.

Mr. Penney worked many long hours each day as a clerk for Mr. Johnson. He toiled just as hard as he would have had he been the owner of the store. He did everything that he would want a clerk to do had he been the owner. He kept the stock in order, took care of the customers courteously, and even swept the floors and sidewalk when they needed sweeping. He was determined to be the kind of clerk that Mr. Johnson would be proud to pay.

Once more he saved his money carefully. This time he had a very special reason for saving it. He wanted to marry Miss Berta Hess, whom he had met while he was living in Longmont. In August, 1899, he and Miss Hess were married in Cheyenne, Wyoming. Following their wedding, he took her to Evanston to live.

Both Mr. Johnson and Mr. Callahan were highly pleased with Mr. Penney and his work. Before long they decided that he was ready to have a Golden Rule Store of his own. They discussed several locations with him and finally settled on Kemmerer, Wyoming. He was eager to manage a store in a small community where he could know his customers well and could thus sell merchandise best suited to their needs.

The store was to be organized on a partnership basis with Mr. Johnson and Mr. Callahan. They estimated that it would take six thousand dollars to buy stock for the store, and that each partner would have to put up two thousand dollars. Young Mr. Penney and his wife invested their savings of five hundred dollars and borrowed the rest from a bank.

Mr. Penney rented a small wooden building as a home for his store. This building was poorly located for getting business and was only twenty-five feet wide and forty-five deep. In order to reach the building, customers would have to leave the concrete sidewalks in the main part of town and follow a wooden sidewalk the rest of the way.

The building had an attic which could be used as a home This attic, about half the size of the store, could be reached by climbing an outside stairs. In the spring of 1902 young Penney and his family, which now included a son named Roswell Kemper, moved into the attic. Their furniture consisted mainly of a pot-bellied stove, cooking utensils, and a bed.

In stocking the store, Mr. Penney used all the empty packing boxes to make shelves for the store or to serve as furniture in the attic. His wife worked hard to help him make the store an attractive place of business.

Before Mr. Penney opened the store, he announced that he planned to sell his merchandise at the lowest prices possible on a cash-and-carry basis. Cash-and-carry selling was new to Kemmerer, because the citizens were used to buying on time. Most of the people round about were either coal miners or ranchers. The coal miners bought much of their merchandise on time at a store operated by the coal mining company.

170

The ranchers had little money to spend except when they sold some of their cattle.

As a young business man, Mr. Penney well remembered how his father and mother had taught him to live by the Golden Rule, "Do unto others as you would have them do unto you." Now in running his store he fully expected to follow this training. He would purchase the best merchandise he could find at reasonable prices and sell it at a small profit.

On April 14, 1902, just as the sun was coming over the horizon, Mr. Penney and his wife opened the new Golden Rule Store for business. They were the only clerks in the store and had to do all the selling. People flocked to the store from both town and country and kept them busy all day long and far into the night.

At midnight Mr. Penney decided that it was time to close the store. He picked up his small son Roswell Kemper, who had been sleeping

in a box beneath the counter. Then, carrying the child in his arms, he joined Mrs. Penney and the two of them climbed the stairs to their attic living quarters.

After they reached the attic, Mrs. Penney piled on the table all the money which they had taken in during the first day and evening. Together they counted the money slowly, penny by penny, nickel by nickel, dime by dime, quarter by quarter, half-dollar by half-dollar, and dollar by dollar. Finally they found that they had taken in a total of four hundred sixty-six dollars and fifty-nine cents.

Mr. Penney reached for a little red notebook which he planned to use as a daily sales record book. On the very first page he wrote: "April 14, 1902, $466.59." He and his wife were far happier than they had expected to be at the end of the first day's business. The Golden Rule Store had started with surprising success.

J. C. Penney Company

MR. PENNEY opened his Golden Rule Store regularly at seven o'clock every morning except Sunday. He kept it open until late at night. As the business grew, he hired a few clerks to help carry on the work.

The new clerks had to be willing to work long hours and to do any and all tasks that were needed to run the store. Besides selling merchandise to customers, they had to keep the stock items neatly put away in boxes or on shelves. They had to dust the counters and shelves and even sweep the floors.

All the clerks were expected to be courteous

to customers and always to treat them fairly. They were supposed to be saving and not to throw anything away, such as boxes, string, and wrapping paper from incoming shipments of goods. These could be used to advantage in wrapping up packages for customers.

Mr. Penney called all the clerks in his store "associates." He expected all these associates to work as diligently for him as he had worked for his employers. He selected his associates just as carefully as he inspected the merchandise for his store. He felt that one was as important as the other.

Within a short time, Mr. Callahan and Mr. Johnson gave Mr. Penney an opportunity to become a partner in stores at Rock Springs, Wyoming, and Cumberland, Wyoming. From then on Mr. Penney not only managed the store at Kemmerer but at both other towns.

While he was busy expanding his business,

a second son, James Cash, Junior, was born. Following his birth, Mr. and Mrs. Penney rented a small house in Kemmerer across the street from the store. Here Mrs. Penney cared for their two small children, but helped in the store when Mr. Penney needed her.

About five years after Mr. Penney opened his Golden Rule Store in Kemmerer, Mr. Johnson and Mr. Callahan offered to sell him their interests in the three stores in Kemmerer, Rock Springs, and Cumberland, for $30,000.00. In addition, they offered to loan him this amount of money with his note as the only guarantee of payment. Even though this offer called for a heavy investment, he and his wife were fully convinced that it would be worthwhile.

Mr. Penney was not content with merely owning three stores. He dreamed of establishing a small chain of Golden Rule Stores on a partnership basis. He believed that managers would be more interested in succeeding, if they had financial investments in the company.

As head of the new chain of Golden Rule Stores, he tried to select managers who were trustworthy and could be trained to accept the principles of honor, confidence, service, and cooperation. Further he encouraged them to purchase one-third interest in their stores, but this was not required.

In 1908, Mr. Penney started new Golden Rule Stores in Bingham, Utah, and in Preston, Idaho. By now he had turned over the management of the Cumberland, Wyoming, store to a young man named Earl Corder Sams. This new manager took a genuine interest in the business and possessed many traits which Mr. Penney liked. Later Mr. Penney said, "I had fifty people working for me before I found Earl Sams."

Finally Mr. Penney decided to offer Mr. Sams an opportunity to start a Golden Rule Store at

Eureka, Utah. In addition, he explained to Mr. Sams that he planned to build up a chain of Golden Rule Stores and invited him to become a third partner in the venture. Mr. Sams accepted and agreed to help expand the chain.

During the next few years the chain of stores grew rapidly. One of the great advantages of the chain was that the stores could purchase merchandise on a cooperative basis, which enabled them to obtain it at lower prices. All the managers continuously looked to Mr. Penney for supervision and assistance.

Mr. Penney had both a personal and financial interest in every store. He traveled regularly from store to store to provide guidance and to answer questions. His guidance ranged from such simple items as keeping stores neat and orderly to such complex problems as determining fair prices and proper methods of selling.

In 1909 Mr. Penney moved his family to Salt

Lake City, Utah, and established headquarters there for his expanding chain of stores. By 1910, only eight years after he had opened his first store at Kemmerer, Wyoming, he directed a chain of fourteen stores.

Late in 1910 Mr. and Mrs. Penney planned to take a belated honeymoon. They had worked together ever since their marriage eleven years before and now looked forward to taking an extended trip to Europe. They planned to leave near the end of the year.

Shortly before they were to leave, Mrs. Penney decided to have her tonsils removed. Following this operation she developed a severe cold which turned into pneumonia. Then, despite every medical assistance possible, nothing could be done to save her.

Following his wife's unexpected death, Mr. Penney passed through a period of great grief and depression. He realized, however, that for

179

the sake of his two sons he must look bravely to the future. During this period he was consoled by a devoted minister who helped him to become engrossed again in his work.

Gradually Mr. Penney's Golden Rule Stores gained a firm foothold in the Rocky Mountain states. Their success led him to develop long-range plans for expansion. In 1913 he decided to incorporate the company under the laws of Utah. The new centralized operations now made it possible to use a uniform system of keeping records, to purchase merchandise on a cooperative basis, and to follow better practices in training managers. All stores continued to operate under the supervision of their managers, as they had from the beginning.

The new company was incorporated in the name of J. C. Penney Company, and from then on the chain of stores operated under Mr. Penney's name. This important change was made for two principal reasons. First, Mr. Penney was the founder and principal owner of the company. Second, certain merchants used the name Golden Rule for their stores, even though they had no connection with Mr. Penney's company or his chain of stores.

By 1914 Mr. Penney was eager to expand his chain of stores into a national chain. In this connection he and Mr. Sams decided to move the company headquarters to New York. Within a few years Mr. Sams was elected President, and Mr. Penney was advanced to Chairman of the Board of Directors. From then on Mr. Penney spent much of his time establishing an educational and training program for the company.

All his life Mr. Penney had regretted that he hadn't acquired more cultural education during his youth. In 1917, while he was helping to prepare an issue of the Company publication, *The Dynamo*, he decided to take time from his business activities to be tutored in literature, arts, philosophy, and music. Thus by diligent study under private tutoring, he obtained much of the formal education that he had missed.

A short time after Mr. Penney moved to New York, he married Mary Kimball, who became a helpful partner. Their married life was of short duration, however, because Mrs. Penney died four years later. She left a son, Kimball, who was named after her family. Now Mr. Penney had three sons to share his sorrow.

By the early 1920's the J. C. Penney Company included hundreds of stores, but Mr. Penney had refrained from starting a store in his home town of Hamilton, Missouri. He refused to compete with his old employer, J. M. Hale. When Mr. Hale decided to retire from business, Mr. Penney purchased his store, remodeled it, and arranged for it to be opened in 1924 as the 500th store in the J. C. Penney Company chain.

As a young man Mr. Penney had chosen merchandising as a career, but he had never lost interest in farming. In 1917 after he became Chairman of the Board of Directors, he decided to engage more and more in outdoor recreational activities for the good of his health. One of his projects included experimenting in various aspects of farming.

As a first large venture, he purchased a farm at Hopewell Junction, New York, to develop a purebred herd of Guernsey cattle, which he called the "Foremost Guernseys." Later he purchased farms in several parts of the country, particularly in Florida, where he acquired one hundred twenty thousand acres. On some farms he experimented with fine breeds of cattle and on others he experimented with horses, mules, hogs, and sheep. In time his research in raising better farm animals attracted wide attention in the field of animal husbandry.

During his period of experimentation and research in farming, he bought his father's original farm along with some extra acreage near Hamilton, Missouri. The house in which he had been born was still standing, but it had been somewhat altered through the years. This property became known as the "Home Place Farm."

Mr. Penney's extensive farm holdings had no financial connection with the J. C. Penney Company. He set up separate corporations and foundations and enlisted support from persons interested in improving farm animals.

In selecting managers for the farms he followed a partnership plan similar to his plan for selecting managers for his stores. He tried to select persons who could be trained to follow the principles of honor, confidence, service, and cooperation. Specifically, he chose managers who attended church regularly and refrained from smoking and drinking.

184

Besides his farming operations, Mr. Penney engaged in several philanthropic projects. In 1926 he founded the Memorial Home Community, now known as the Penney Retirement Home, at Penney Springs, Florida, for the use of religious workers and their families. In another project, Mr. Penney provided financial aid for the religious magazine, *Christian Herald*.

During this same year he married Caroline Autenrieth, who was destined to become an important helpmate during the remainder of his life. They had two daughters, Mary Frances and Carol. Then Mr. Penney had a total of three sons and two daughters.

When the Great Depression came in 1929 and the early '30's, Mr. Penney suffered great personal financial losses from the failure of several New York banks. He already had borrowed heavily to finance his philanthropic projects. Now he needed money to continue them.

185

In order to borrow money, he had to use some of his personal stock in the J. C. Penney Company as security or collateral. As the stock decreased in value, he had to put up more and more. By 1931 he had lost part of the fortune that he had struggled so hard to accumulate.

With the help of his wife he faced these adverse conditions bravely. They dismissed many of their servants and took over much of the work on their country estate at White Plains, where they lived part of the year. She helped in the house and he on the grounds.

During the Great Depression, when Mr. Penney was fifty-six years old, he made a business trip to Battle Creek, Michigan. While there he became seriously ill and was placed in a sanitarium, as a result of worrying over his financial problems. He lost the will to live and one night even wrote farewell notes to members of his family. The next morning he overheard a group of patients singing the old familiar hymn, "God Will Take Care of You." He hobbled to join the patients, who were holding a prayer meeting. He began to pray and suddenly felt released from the nervous tension that had been torturing him. Now once more he had the will to live and to carry on important activities as before.

Ever since the J. C. Penney Company had been incorporated in 1909, he never had accepted a salary from the company. For income he had depended entirely on the earnings from his stock in the company. After he had suffered financially, the company started to pay him a salary. Also, through the help of his brother Herbert and a few friends, he was able to buy back much of his stock in the company.

In later life Mr. Penney still took a keen personal interest in the company stores. He had a special reputation for visiting stores unannounced. Once when a store manager arrived in the morning to open his store, he found Mr. Penney sweeping the sidewalk in front of the store. On another occasion Mr. Penney paused as he was walking through a store to show a clerk how to wrap a shirt more neatly.

As Mr. Penney traveled about, he derived great pleasure from meeting people not connected with his stores. Once he attended a state fair and sat down beside a young "Future Farmer" to talk with him about his prize-winning Guernsey calf. During World War II he allowed the Waves, or young women in the Navy, to use the Penney stores as recruiting stations.

Throughout his busy life, Mr. Penney always found time to visit his hometown of Hamilton, Missouri, where he kept up many friendships through the years. He even purchased a house there which he rented to the manager of his store except for a room which he kept for himself. He made many contributions to his hometown of

Hamilton. He gave financial assistance in constructing a high school and public library. He felt that everyone should have an opportunity to improve educationally and culturally.

Throughout life Mr. Penney was a very impressive person, who attracted attention. He had a gracious manner, a gentle voice, and a pleasant smile which caused people to enjoy meeting him or even seeing him. Frequently people about the country would be heard saying, "I talked with the great Mr. Penney today," or "I met the great Mr. Penney today."

In 1958 Mr. Penney resigned as Chairman of the Board of Directors of the J. C. Penney Company, but he continued to serve as a member of the Board. From this time on he regularly worked in his offices on the 45th floor of the Penney building in New York and kept up close connections with the company. During his later years he had a summer home at Greens Farms, near Westport, Connecticut, and an apartment on Park Avenue in New York. Regardless of which home he occupied, he continued to be driven regularly each morning to his office.

Reporters always enjoyed visiting with Mr. Penney because they found him both courteous and highly informed. He willingly pictured for them the rigorous experiences of his childhood and early business endeavors which played such an important part in his successful career. He also contributed authentic information by writing articles for religious journals and by writing and collaborating in writing several books.

Penney's success story is the story of a man who chose to build a business on integrity. In recognition of his achievement in developing a huge chain of department stores, his contributions to better farming, and his philanthropic activities, he was the recipient of many special awards and honorary degrees.

On Saturday, September 12, 1970, Mrs. Penney held a mammoth reception for Mr. Penney at Greens Farms to celebrate his approaching ninety-fifth birthday on September 16. For two hours this spry, vivacious, and extremely happy merchant prince stood in line with his wife to greet more than five hundred personal friends and relatives.

By now his brother Herbert, his sister Pearl and his son James Cash had died, but his sister Letha, now Mrs. Roy Ott, and his two sons and two daughters were there with their families.

This was one of the final events in the life of James Cash Penney. A few months later he suffered injuries in a fall and died on February 12, 1971, as a result of complications. Thus ended the career of a famous American who built a mighty business enterprise based on the principles of the Golden Rule.

More About This Book

WHEN J. C. PENNEY LIVED

1875   J. C. PENNEY WAS BORN NEAR HAMILTON, MIS-
        SOURI, ON SEPTEMBER 16.

There were thirty-seven states in the Union.

Ulysses S. Grant was President.

The population of the country was about
44,355,000.

1875–   JIMMY LIVED WITH HIS FAMILY AND ATTENDED
1893   SCHOOL IN HAMILTON.

Alexander Graham Bell invented the telephone,
1876.

Thomas Edison invented the electric light bulb,
1876.

F. W. Woolworth established his first five and
ten cent store, 1880.

Sears, Roebuck Company was organized, 1886.

Thomas Edison invented the motion picture
machine, 1889.

1893–
1902
JIMMY WORKED IN A DRY GOODS STORE IN HAM-
ILTON, THEN MOVED WEST FOR HIS HEALTH.

Grover Cleveland was President, 1893-1897.

Severe business depression began, throwing
many people out of work, 1893.

Henry Ford built his first automobile, 1897.

Spanish-American War was fought, 1898.

1903–
1913
YOUNG PENNEY OPENED HIS FIRST STORE AND
FOUNDED A CHAIN OF GOLDEN RULE STORES.

Wilbur and Orville Wright flew the first
heavier-than-air aircraft, 1903.

The Ford Motor Company was organized, 1903.

Robert Peary discovered the North Pole, 1909.

Woodrow Wilson was President, 1913-1921.

1913–
1971
J. C. PENNEY COMPANY WAS FOUNDED AND GREW
RAPIDLY OVER THE YEARS.

Regular radio broadcasts were begun, 1920.

Stock market prices crashed and a severe business depression followed, 1929.

World War II was fought, 1941-1945.

The United Nations Charter was adopted, 1945.

1971   J. C. PENNEY DIED AT HIS HOME IN CONNECTI-
        CUT AT THE AGE OF 96.

There were fifty states in the Union.

Richard M. Nixon was President.

The population of the country was about 205,570,000.

DO YOU REMEMBER?

1. What work did Jimmy, Elie, and Mittie do when they went to the farm with Mr. Penney?

2. What difficulty did Jimmy have when he first started to school?

3. What special responsibility did Jimmy have to assume when he was eight years old?

4. How did Jimmy manage to secure odd jobs in the neighborhood to earn money?

5. What problem did Jimmy face when he purchased a new pair of shoes?

6. How did Jimmy make a profit by raising a pig in the back yard?

7. Why did Jimmy become disturbed about the price he paid for firewood?

8. Why did Jimmy have to sell the little mare which he purchased?

9. Why did Mr. Penney make Jimmy stop selling watermelons outside the fairgrounds?

10. How did Jimmy get his first experience in the merchandising business?

11. How did young Mr. Penney build up a chain of Golden Rule Stores?

12. Why was the name of the chain changed to the J. C. Penney Company?

13. What financial problems did Mr. Penney face during the Great Depression?

14. What interesting projects did Mr. Penney carry on in the later years of his life?

IT'S FUN TO LOOK UP THESE THINGS

1. What did Jimmy's father mean by wanting him to become self-reliant?

2. What are some of the most common jobs that boys can do to earn money?

3. How does a dry goods store differ from other kinds of stores?

4. Why is it important for a store to be kept neat and orderly?

5. What is the Golden Rule which Mr. Penney used for guidance in founding his stores?

6. What other great chains of stores were founded early in the present century?

INTERESTING THINGS YOU CAN DO

1. Draw a map to show in what part of the country J. C. Penney lived as a boy.

2. Describe the duties of a store manager and explain why these duties are important.

3. Tell what is meant by the different departments in a store.

4. Explain the terms "profit" and "loss" with which business persons are concerned.

5. Visit a J. C. Penney store and report interesting sights to the class.

6. Make a list of other big chains of stores besides the J. C. Penney Company.

7. Describe interesting projects which J. C. Penney carried on to help others.

OTHER BOOKS YOU MAY ENJOY READING

A. P. Giannini: Boy of San Francisco, Marie Hammontree. Trade and School Editions, Bobbs-Merrill.

Jim Penney's Golden Nugget, Elizabeth P. Withridge. Abingdon.

John Wanamaker: Boy Merchant, Olive W. Burt. Trade and School Editions, Bobbs-Merrill.

Mr. Penney, Harry Albers. Eerdmans.

The Peddlers, Leonard Everett Fisher. Watts.

Your Career in Selling, Robert A. Liston. Messner.

INTERESTING WORDS IN THIS BOOK

abrupt (ă brŭpt′) : sudden, without warning

accumulate (ă kū′mū lāt) : acquire, collect

assume (ă sūm′) : take on, adopt

bolt (bōlt) : long roll of cloth

canvass (kăn′vás) : go about asking or looking for something

collateral (kō lăt′ĕr ăl) : something of value put up to guarantee the payment of a loan

corrupt (kŏ rŭpt′) : make evil or wicked

courteous (kûr′tĕ ŭs) : polite, well-mannered

cradle (krā′d′l) : scythe with a frame attached to the blade that catches the falling stalks of grain and causes them to lie flat

dasher (dăsh′ĕr) : movable bladed part of a churn which agitates the cream and turns it to butter

definite (dĕf′ĭ nĭt) : clear, unmistakable in meaning

diagnosis (dī′ăg nō′sĭs) : decision reached following a careful study of facts

diligent (dĭl′ĭ jĕnt) : industrious

dire (dīr) : extreme

elder (ĕl′dĕr) : one of the governing officers of a church

estimate (ĕs′tĭ māt) : form an opinion as to the size or cost of something

forge (fôrj) : blacksmith's open furnace, where metal is heated and softened

foundation (foun dā′shŭn) : organization that has been granted money to perform certain duties

gracious (grā′shŭs) : polite, charming and agreeable

gunny sack (gŭn′ĭ săk) : sack made of heavy woven jute, used for holding heavy materials

halter (hôl'tĕr) : rope or strap used for leading a farm animal, as a horse or cow

incorporate (ĭn kôr'pȯ rāt) : form a legal organization, registered with the government

investment (ĭn vĕst' mĕnt) : employment of money in a product or service to earn more money

instep (ĭn'stĕp) : top of the human foot between the ankle and the toes

interfere (ĭn'tĕr fēr') : get in the way of, conflict with

mortgage (môr'gĭj) : claim on property given in return for borrowed money

philanthropic (fĭl'ăn thrŏp'ĭk) : charitable, having to do with charity

project (prŏj'ĕkt) : plan or undertaking

rant (rănt) : talk noisily and excitedly

rigorous (rĭg'ēr ŭs) : harsh, severe

scythe (sīth) : tool with a long handle and a long curved blade, used for cutting standing grains and grass

self-reliant (sĕlf rė lī'ănt) : able to take care of one's self

sickle (sĭk''l) : curved metal blade with short handle, used for cutting grass

vivacious (vī vā'shŭs) : lively, spirited and gay

200

Childhood

OF FAMOUS AMERICANS

CHILDHOOD
OF FAMOUS
AMERICANS